*Remember when the only
bicycle riders you saw
were little kids — and
maybe old women with funny
hats in English movies?*

Well, those days are over now. Today you'll
see men in bowler hats making better time
on bikes than in Caddys in midtown traffic.
You'll see parks closed off to the pollution-
spouting horseless carriages while cyclists
discover what clear air is all about. You'll
see students deciding that it's a better idea
to get back in touch with the world around
them than to whiz through life behind a
car's window glass. You'll see men and
women of all ages finding out that their
bodies are good for something besides
pushing starter buttons, and that the more
they use those bodies, the better they get.

The *Clear Creek Bike Book* is the book
for all of them — and for you as well.

Other SIGNET Books of Special Interest

☐ **WHAT YOU SHOULD KNOW BEFORE YOU HAVE YOUR CAR REPAIRED by Anthony Till.** Get the facts on the Great American Repair Racket! This book can save you big money the next time you need any kind of work done on your car. It includes a special "Flat-Rate Book" to show how much you should pay for all major and minor car repair jobs. (#N5087—$1.00)

☐ **HOW INTELLIGENT ARE YOU? by Victor Serebriakoff.** Intelligence testing has become increasingly important in modern society and the person who *knows himself* and his capabilities will certainly be ahead of the game. Why not take the opportunity to test yourself with this book so that the next time somebody tells you, "Oh, you think you're so smart;" you can tell them just how smart you are! (#Q5062—95¢)

☐ **THE COMPLETE BOOK OF CAMPING by Heywood Gould.** Before you go off into the wilderness to face the nightmare of the "bungled vacation," learn just what you're getting into and what you'll need to cope with it. This complete guide tells you where to go, what to take, and how to deal with the different hazards you'll meet along the way. (#N5051—$1.00)

☐ **BITE: A New York Restaurant Strategy by Gael Greene.** This is a very special kind of restaurant guide for those who delight in being raked over the coals by New York's expensive, snobbish and sometimes not so good restaurant scene, or those who will stop at no lengths to beat the system. BITE presents a rare, fascinating and hilarious look at New York's stomachs, egos and some of its most expensive little insanities. (#W5010—$1.50)

THE
Clear Creek
Bike Book

by
Hal Aigner, Bob Jensen, Charles Powers,
and Lucky Wentworth,
with additional material by
Peter Lawlor and *Clear Creek* Editors

A SIGNET BOOK
NEW AMERICAN LIBRARY
TIMES MIRROR

SIGNET TRADEMARK REG. U.S. PAT. OFF. AND FOREIGN COUNTRIES
REGISTERED TRADEMARK — MARCA REGISTRADA
HECHO EN CHICAGO, U.S.A.

First Signet Printing, March, 1973

2 3 4 5 6 7 8 9

PRINTED IN THE UNITED STATES OF AMERICA

Contents

Acknowledgments

FIRST, to others who have written about bicycles: Eugene Sloane, *The Complete Book of Bicycling,* Trident Press, 1971; Tom Cuthbertson, *Anybody's Bicycle Book,* Ten Speed Press, 1971; *The Bicycle Book,* Earth Action Council, UCLA Alumni Association, 1971; *Bicycling Magazine,* San Francisco; and Colin Fletcher, *The Complete Walker,* Alfred Knopf, 1968. Also, to supportive organizations like the League of American Wheelmen and the British Cycling Federation, and to the proprietors of the Stanyan Street Cyclery, San Francisco.

For photographs, we wish to thank Roger Lubin and Hank Lebo; for graphics, Jon Goodchild; for diagrams, Joe Holmes; for editorial assistance, Pennfield Jensen and Bill Barich; for typing and endurance, Lorrie Tetzlaff; and, for odd jobs and fine camaraderie, the Clear Creek staff.

Introduction

ON OCCASION the world seems to have gone absolutely bananas. We destroy Hopi shrines thousands of years old to fire a power plant with coal so that the neon lights and mindless sprawl of Los Angeles can continue unimpeded. A total of 80 percent of the people live on 2 percent of the land area, yet Americans use 60 percent of the world's resources while only comprising 7 percent of its population. In a way it all becomes symbolized by the automobile. So you make a decision to do something, but what? The road to sanity can begin with the purchase of a bicycle.

Stepping outside the insular, vinyl obesity of a Cougar, Stingray, Fury, Toronado, or other Detroit Dodo, one buys a bicycle and is reunited with the environment. The rider breathes *air,* such as it is; he smells *aromas,* such as they are; and he feels the planet turning beneath him in the texture of the road.

A winding road blessed with cyclists has been liberated. Cyclists are naturally spare and meaningful, two very desirable virtues; and for their tastes, getting there is as much or more fun than arriving. That's what separates and ennobles them.

Though cycling is, of course, not the source of character, it certainly nurtures the human spirit. A cyclist, without fail, knows where he's been, has seen what the landscape is like, and can make knowledgeable comments about both. He is a good companion, a find in this day when people seem to have forgotten *how* to be friendly, or even *why* they should be. Anonymous ciphers in bellicose bureaucracies, people have lost the sense of companionship in struggle. The first fresh flush of comaraderie that once characterized the nation has fallen before the reduction to dollars of virtually every aspect of American life.

Nothing worthwhile seems to be *made* anymore except money. Things are just produced, bought, and thrown away with seemingly the sole motivation of bringing that process as close to one single motion as possible. Existence ends up being inexorably linked to dollars, and people who live just to make money are the most deadly and boring in the world.

Fortunately there is hope. There are better things to be made than money and its bedfellow, war. There is love and the prospect of a better world. Many of the people who are trying to make that new world are starting out with bicycles. The purchase of a pedaling machine and the consistent delight that comes from it may be the best solution yet devised to ease air pollution and restore health to weakening bodies.

Consider just these few points. The fossil fuel consumption of bicycles is notoriously low; what a blow to strike against oil barons. Since excess weight is a detriment to the machine, as little metal as is safe is used in its construction. There is not enough rubber on all the bikes in the world worth fighting a war over in Southeast Asia, or anywhere else.

To become the owner of a bicycle, wending one's way in strategic and moral victory through rush-hour traffic, or even just trekking through the back roads of the planet, is to become a member of an extensive fraternity. Most bicyclists are, by necessity, friends. They get into trouble, something goes wrong on the roads, they know who they can lean on . . . another cyclist.

Which is why we have put together *The Clear Creek Bike Book*. Not only a guide to purchasing, repairing, and maintaining a machine, it is a compendium of experience. Each of the several authors of the work brings a special knowledge to the art of cycling. In fact, when Jeffrey Weiss from The New American Library asked me if Clear Creek would produce a book on bicycling, we had already published one bicycle article (reprinted here) and had more in the works. The opportunity of presenting the essays in the context of this book has been infinitely more exciting.

Peter Lawlor, whose articles are equaled only by his knowledge of the noble art of brewing and consuming ale and stout, had already promised a superb story on no more than the promise of pay and the bribe of a four-pack of Guinness. Charlie Powers materialized one day in a blue nylon sleeping bag strategically located on my back lawn in Berkeley, California, having pedaled from Bethesda, Maryland, to visit an old college roommate, Bob Jensen. Within days the place looked like Miracle Willie's Bicycle Parts Paradise and their chapter on bicycle riding and mechanics is a lucid and direct approach to solving the most basic and common bicycle tragedies — an invaluable aid to any self-sufficient cyclist.

Marchant ("Lucky") Wentworth is the resident bicycle guru at the Washington Ecology Center in Washington, D.C. Overseer of all things mechanical and political, he is also a genuine bicycle radical as his chapter, "The Politics of Bicycling," will demonstrate. Scholarly, subtle, and dryly humorous, Hal Aigner is the continuity man. A writer by profession and a laborer by necessity, Hal happened to answer his Mill Valley telephone with a yes and I said, "You're hired." He has taken his special interest in bicycles to the fields of history and lore, health and safety, and wielded the crucial red pencil as chief editor.

In many ways *The Clear Creek Bike Book* is an organized discussion by several good friends of every aspect of bicycling. We feel that way. We hope that after reading this, you will too.

—*Pennfield Jensen*

1 *Meditation*

PETER LAWLOR

Part One

In the beginning and at the end are time and space. How to move through two dimensions and not miss the magic? Slowly, quietly, with predatory eye and mammal grace. No speed but what you supply, your own energy redirected, foot to pedal, sinew-popping good feel. Eventually, a rhythm grows to glide by on, freeing your self to observe, to see. Nothing between you and the pulsating world but an invisible curtain of air. Part of the cycle while you ride your cycle.

Peter Lawlor is an ale maker and a man who perpetuates grand traditions. His affection for bicycles parallels the love a man might have for a pet animal, and with that spirit, he offers the following meditation.

For a very good reason, I never lost my faith in bikes. And that formed quite a while ago. Not everybody had cars then.

I can remember my first bicycle, a BSA, bought in response to an ad. The first feeling of the smooth handlebars—it was a superb charge on my fingers. It had an Eadie coaster rear hub, which enabled one to pedal backward to apply the brake; a Brooks saddle that I polished to stop the rain from stretching it. And it had a carbide lamp. That's the kind that dripped water onto carbide blocks making a combustible gas. I used to go for rides after school and leave it under the bushes while I went for a swim.

Later on I got a motorcycle that lived a short life, and because it nearly terminated my existence, I never got another. Then I got stuck with cars in order to make a living. But the reason I never lost faith in bikes is because they never changed face nor frame. My bicycle of thirty-five years ago had the same outline as the ones of today.

Americans throw themselves into each new craze with an abandon that staggers the world. The people of Copenhagen, who have been bicycling to work for years, couldn't picture our overnight awakening here: new bike shops opening up weekly, frantic bike paths going in, signs reading Bicycle Path everywhere (many quite inappropriate), ten-year-olds with ten-speeders, city dumps full of old bikes, only new bikes in use, housewives hurriedly learning to balance, old men with paunches pedaling gloriously for a few blocks then subsiding in a sweat, braces of bikes perched on racks of sports cars heading off to some Elysian trail, husband and wife matched sets.

Bikes, bikes, bikes — always the best and most elaborate. Bikes at discount houses, bikes at Abercrombie and Fitch. Your exclusive custom bicycle dealer ready to monogram; take your weight, ability, age, celestial sign; and tie it all into a personalized bike. National Bike Day. Bikes Are Beautiful buttons in L.A.; Bike for a Better City in New York.

It is all accomplished overnight in our frantic, optimistic, brash way of doing things. Our striving for the overall panacea. And then always someone making money on it.

And in Amsterdam, unimpressed and unaltered, erect in the saddle, the businessman pedals his one-speed ancient, and the winds of our excitement will never unsettle his poise.

Where will our sudden spurt get us?

Will the joggers, cyclists, backpackers, walkers, and watchers be allotted a quiet path alongside the ribbon of cement?

It is interesting to speculate, because biking is a total reversal of all the energies of the large forces that built our economy. It is a matter of being able to foster, and even find, a place for smaller and quieter types of activities — activities in which there appears to be relatively less money to be made. In a few years' time, it would not only change our outlook, it could vastly change our economy.

What is being done for us bikeniks? How do we stack up? When the inherent superiority of the bicycle has been demonstrated, as in Chicago recently when it was pitted against an automobile and a bus over a four-mile course in heavy traffic — bus, fifty-four minutes; auto, thirty-one minutes; the cycle, a mere nineteen minutes — then bikes begin to do things for us.

The National Bureau of Outdoor Recreation has a recommendation of twenty-five miles of bicycling trails for each community of fifty thousand residents. Since the first "Safety Routes" were opened in Florida in 1962, the Sunshine State's cities have taken steps and marked off bike routes. Milwaukee has sixty-four miles of routes exclusively for bikes. Marin County, California, which boasts the largest bicycling clubs in the country, has sixty-five miles of marked trail through some of the loveliest rolling countryside you could hope to see.

The most encouraging sign so far that I see is the Smithsonian Plan, which will set up a series of radical bike arteries in Washington, D.C., and this is not just a sideline but actually allowing the bicycle to take its place alongside the car — David against Goliath, bikes against Detroit.

For my part I'll take on the gas burners anytime. With a combination of bike-cum-ferry swing, I can beat the Greyhound bus hands down from San Francisco's ferry building across the Golden Gate to Mill Valley on the other side of the bay. And downtown, while some poor guy is circling the blocks to find a parking space, I've been to my destination, completed business, and had time for a quickie in the local pub.

The politicians are not only involved in bikes, but are also on them. That means things will happen. In Sacramento, where there is a bikeway all the way from State College to the Capitol, the senators ride their bikes and have spaces reserved for bike racks on the Capitol grounds, which were formerly marked for car parking. One of the main cross streets in town is set to become exclusively for bikes.

The bike is a convenient, undemanding vehicle that, by its quietness — unbetrayed by storage space, temperament, noise, fuel consumption, or expense problems — is able to keep a close secret.

These and many other things are a bike:

On an expedition it is a friend to hang things on.

It can support the tent when there are no branches.

It is a useful weapon.

It can be dismounted and flailed at menacing dogs, and ridden fast to outdistance short-legged ones.

It can be used to taunt police.

A bull in a field will not charge a bike.

Without a penny in your pocket, a bike is collateral for imminent needs.

It is hockable, God forbid.

An adventurer with a bike can pass the hat to get himself around the world.

A bike can carry as much as a mule.

A bike equipped with paddles and floats is a boat.

A bike devoid of wheels and placed on a stand is a flab reducer.

An old bike wheel is a clothesline. It can be used as a manual rotisserie for grilling hamburgers.

All of these good things is a bike.

But best of all, a bike helps keep alive the spirit of secret adventure.

I have several of these secrets hidden in various places.

I keep a bicycle in San Francisco.

It is pure white to go with the ambiance of the city's mission houses; the ones on Dolores Street where the loveliest mission is. It goes well with the similar look of the Marina.

It is pure and bold, having ten speeds with a well-geared-down alpine for the sudden hills. It is jaunty for sprints along the Marina and the Embarcadero.

I call it my white charger because it is a knight-errant sort of machine that has been to peace marches, has carried supplies to beleaguered damsels—namely, my daughter stranded in Santa Cruz—and has broken the resistance of police patrolling the Golden Gate Bridge in the old no-cycling days.

With all this, I keep a hefty lock on it because I have lost three in San Francisco and each thief took a part of my life. Though fierce with resentment at the time, I begrudge nothing now because I know someone is enjoying them. One of these was a Negini, a sample model of an Italian superlight weight. It was so exotic I had to adjust it after every trip. A crosswind would carry it out from under me, it was so light; and the wheels and tires so delicate and balanced they were cut to ribbons on the fine glass of discarded beer bottles.

For all that, I really loved it and I wonder if the new owner can carry the sentiment.

The most I have lost from my white charger was the front

wheel. The rest was securely chained to a bike stand. There it was, all down in front, forks sticking into the ground. A suspicious little boy was hanging around. I resorted to a miserable trick, feeling that he had seen the operation, and offered him a quarter if he could give me a clue. He pointed to the bushes and ran.

I did get back the wheel minus a few bits and pieces, though I never did find out if he was the culprit.

Since that time, when dismounted, I have kept my steed in a prominent place away from converging crowds, certainly away from parking lots, and, if possible, within eyesight; and if I have to go inside, I try to make sure someone who is working in the vicinity can see it. If one lock is useless and two locks still a chance, then public surveillance might do it. Sad to say, the purity of my white bike doesn't deter the blackhearted.

The charger is a favorite bike because I have ridden most of the California highway coast route number one on it, including several times to Big Sur, where the hills have inspired and all but killed me, and well north past Mendocino with a southwest tail wind that almost flew me to Oregon but beat me into an old man on the way back. I couldn't sell that bike, so I left it with a good friend on Russian Hill who promised me he would have the wheels trued and ride it to work. That's a good bargain. It will always be there.

I have a secret bike in New Zealand.

It is strung up against the wall of my dad's garage. For many years it remained there looking doggy and rusting away. I was back there a few years ago and pulled it down. For want of anything better to do, I took it to pieces; scraped, primed, and painted it; bought new grips and a racy two-tone saddle. I put in a lot of time on it for one reason only — it was the only reason I didn't dismember it and stick it in the dustbin — it was my first bike.

Damn stupid to hang onto an old bike. It is like keeping old skis. They are obsolete and don't run as well as the new ones. If they need fixing and are taken into a shop, the repairman is going to be insulted. Repairmen do not have any sentimentality. "It will cost you so much to fix you might as well buy a new one," rattles one mechanic's tongue.

Anyway, I did fix it up, justifying the sentiments with the

fact that it was an old BSA, which is rare now, and the fact that it had an old Eadie coaster hub, which you backpedaled to brake, the brake shoe a superb hunk of copper ring that expanded against the outside drum of chrome steel. It was practical too because the area was flat for fifty miles around and the one speed of medium range was simple, even if I did feel like Prince Albert on that old chopper.

Recently I got a letter from my dad, concerned because someone had broken into the garage and taken down the bike and removed a tire. What should I do about it?

Well, I couldn't fly out and right the matter – a mere business of $700 round trip. But I did respond to his concern and airmailed instructions: "Tie it up again and cover it with a sack. Take off wheels. Strip tires and put them in a bag."

The dismembered body has not since been tampered with, and I rather doubt if even I'll have the guts to put that one together again.

Although I do not have a bike in Amsterdam, I almost did. Fortunately, there is someone pedaling happily on it now, that is, if it hasn't run itself into the canals, which is the natural death for bikes in that city.

It was a rental. I took it for the day from a chap on a barge. It was a Friday and I had forgotten that barges and others in business on the canals usually weekend binge. By night, life on the barge was dead for the weekend, and I was stuck with the bike and only a short time before my plane was ready to leave. But I got to know Amsterdam – the whackiest cycling city in the world.

The first sight of Amsterdam looks like the dumping ground of all the world's two-wheelers. The city provides a free bike for anyone caught short. You will see them anywhere and they stand out because they are painted white. Sometimes sloppily so, as if some city painter had lined them up and did a hit-and-miss job with a whitewash brush. You ask no one, just jump on, go where you are going, and prop it up against a wall. Someone will use it again in a few days. These machines are really heavy looking – Queen Wilhelmina jobs – and no one in his right mind would want to steal them. There is another public bike painted green. Don't use these as they are for the military.

Naturally, time and weather wear down ownerless bikes pretty fast, and their only graveyard is the canal. When they have done their work, they collapse slowly into the canals, pulled down by rust and the sheer weight of chain guards, old lamps, and thick rubber pedals.

The rest of this great assemblage of bikes, two and three deep against the city's buildings, sorts itself out as the commuters pile out of work. Most of them are unlocked, which contributes to a certain type of bicycle thief peculiar to Amsterdam, the skid row opportunist, who clears them in whole or in part for a few guilders to keep himself in gin. With this confusion of bikes, it is hard to track down the culprit.

They say in Copenhagen nobody steals a bike. What moral this points out I don't know.

I joined with the Amsterdam cyclists in their bewildering traffic code. They sit tall in the saddle, which is much lower than the front handlebars and which rises out of a stem so long it is easy to hang groceries or a briefcase on the bars without touching the front wheel. They must have backpedal brakes rather than levers to keep hands free for signaling or, the further touch of elegance, the umbrella in one hand.

The racers are another local breed who dress in track suits and reversed painter's hats and keep to the fast lanes. They are incredibly tough and have no truck with the city commuters.

I finally did catch my bargee after thoughts of packaging up the bike to take it aboard the plane. It happened I made a fairly large deposit and I would have sent him the balance. Sweaty and singleted, he welcomed me back after his binge, apologizing and only charging me for the one day. "Come in and have a schnapps," he said, wanting to give me details of his carousing, but I only had a few minutes before the plane left.

I keep a stable of bikes in my garage in England. The first one is orange and black in the sort of earthy colors you find in the country tweeds. It is not a knight-errant sort of machine like my white one. It is a very genteel type. To keep it company, I bought another one, cheap, at an auction and have been a month rebuilding it. Under the old paint, I discovered a blue blood so it is a fitting companion to the one in tweeds.

The labor of love in rebuilding from a good light angular-looking frame is worth it alone. It takes me forever because every time I go into my friendly corner cycle dealer to get a missing nut, we become involved in long talks. Absorbed, too, in all the appendages that English repair shops stock, I could go on forever fitting new bits. This brace of gentlemanly bikes sports mudguards, cut away in front and full in the rear, so as to have something to fix an adequate reflector to and also to present a formidable rear when riding two abreast on a Sunday. The multitude of friends who drop in necessitates me keeping this pair in readiness. Somehow it seems that American visitors to England expect bikes to be on tap at all times.

I may have to sell this pedigree pair when I leave. They will continue on proudly because there is good stock here.

Part Two

Lawlor has traveled to many an odd and distant point on the globe, seeking the almost mystical experience to be found in the proper combination of movement and vision.

Full satisfaction is not always guaranteed, however, as this tale of a ride to the fabled Stonehenge will reveal, but since getting there is as enjoyable as arriving, all is never lost.

"Its center stone by some extraordinary skill or magic is said to be precisely touched by the rising sun on midsummer morning," read the travel note. No great discovery ever came out of a brochure. Because it said midsummer I felt perversely that the secret lay with the solstice at the other end of the calendar.

At the town of Exeter the day before midwinter, studying a highly colored map in an extremely confused state of mind, shuffling around looking for reprieve, I know it will not come. The deep green was the high elevations blending into light green down the grades. White for the low valleys – good. But those brown nobs – high desolation.

Ninety miles divided by the circumference of a wheel gives

the number of revolutions to the famed cromlech. But it was motherish cold and the Devon soil raised itself in spires in the black frost.

This was a pilgrimage.

The morning sun quickened on the pedals and I felt like yelling to the coated huddled freaks. "Man, this is it forever!" They might have picked up the strain.

I did laugh in the road-close faces of two furred thumbed-up hippies. Their slow smile stayed with me for many miles. Then a man-mad idiot doing a Stirling Moss with a wide roaring sweep around a truck on a two-lane uphill stretch broke the spell.

Oh why do you create misery? I could see it on your face.

The first morale comes strong. Mainly in the seat of my pants. But it is in the hands too and the song part is in the pedals. It is a three-point suspension and those are the main points you have to watch. "The all-important handlebar and saddle," says *British Cycling Manual*. With these in fine adjustment, the rest can take care of itself. If the car driver has a problem, he's stuck inside with it.

I was passing Sidmouth after twelve miles of the up-and-down stuff and here was this monument. I couldn't believe it. Damn pity there wasn't a soul around to share it with except those buzzing Moss fellows. Literally it went: "On this spot after watching the glorious sunset of Aug 3rd 1904 Thomas Gilbert Smith M.D. fell dead from his bicycle. Thunder and lightning immediately followed. His motto in life was 'Do and Dare.'"

I don't know if it was the motto or the glorious sunset bit that got me but I could see old Smith toppling off, his penny-farthing sparks flying out of his ears. Lightning or a coronary — it was beyond me.

Farther on, another one of those anachronisms — a snack truck in this land of brick tearooms! I was almost tempted but knew his tea wouldn't be too good and his coffee unspeakably lousy. Then I saw his number plate and it said DAD with three digits following and I couldn't bear that.

So I keep going to Ilminster, sweeping into the marketplace with my red fluorescent Windbreaker and orange bike totally upsetting the locals. That might have been just because I had turned fifty summers a while ago and the hair was wild to my shoulders.

A fine pub was where to splice the main brace. One rum because I was shaking so. No beer, dear, unless it's going to be an easy day. It rubbers the legs so—and that comes out of no manual.

This was a pilgrimage.

I had a pot of hot pot to follow. I would recommend this to Everyman on his trip from Exeter to Stonehenge. That pot was so hot that I tipped it onto the plate and the steam from that operation warmed my hands and half the pub. All over these isles the working lads joyously eat this. The names never disguise the contents. It is potatoes and mutton boiled with veggies, seldom known as stew. A quick jetter on a twenty-one-day charter fooled twice by words condemns forever the cooks.

This one happened to be called hot pot because it was cooked in an earthenware pot. If the top gets a browning, it is called shepherd's pie. Give it some Worcestershire sauce. Give it a chance. The Irish give it a good talking to.

From Devon into Somerset, and only an hour there in the thin end of the shire. Then into mysterious Dorset and no unctuous signs anywhere to say how proud everyone was to have me. All quite dignified. Very Thomas Hardyish in Dorset with things underneath.

Two small villages with names to play with. First Zere, as if to say in the local dialect, "It's here." But I saw nothing so I didn't stop. Then Mere, which might be saying nothing much or "Merely this," and if you can't see it at once, why bother? It is an old word for lake and I saw no lake. Mere is hidden.

Mere twists and turns secretively into a marketplace. It has the best inn signs I've ever seen—strange beasts rampant. Halfway from Exeter to London, the coaches stopped here. Greatcoated and tall booted, the Hardy and Austin characters are only shadows in the doorways but they are there.

Stay here easily for your first night, Everyman. The coaches took much longer than a bike.

I went on pushing it needlessly—repeating Zere and Mere and Where?

The map must have been off a bit or I had misjudged the light and dark bits. The hills kept on coming. A corner always helped and the trucks sucking at the air mightily gave a friendly pull. No one direction for long and the road signs made it into snakes and ladders — miss a turn, back to go, on to fifty. The little places went by church-and-a-pub-church-and-a-pub like the song of a train. Never a straight road. I kept on thinking of Chesterton's verse because it is the only way to sum up the roads:

> Before the Romans came to Rye
> Or out to Severn strode,
> The rolling English drunkard
> Made the rolling English road

What a picture! An original hair — something B.C., with a skin cloak tossed across the shoulders, making the early tracks as he weaved on to Salisbury in his rawhide thongs with some potent fire, God knows how concocted, that kept him going. In his memory no one throws out bottles and empty beer cans.

(It is lonely not to be able to read all the beer labels as I did to while the miles away in the U.S.A. And remembering not quite so quaintly the increasing carpet of scattered glass near the bigger towns.)

Bless the old ancient tippler. His meanderings keep the traffic to a kindly pace for me and even the sports addict swinging the swathe is more noise than speed. I can hear him in time to dodge.

Then some black dart shot across the sky aimed at some somber bull's-eye. The short dark midwinter day was over in dark Dorset and that jet could have been anything. And thus exposed to the UFOs I started to look for a bed-and-breakfast place.

There was a man asleep in his little helpful roadside shack and with a sign that said you could join up here. I wasn't going to join up in any war, but realizing that this is the automobile club, my hand went instinctively to the AAA card in my wallet. Anyway he was so keen to help I didn't need it: it was like being back home. I got a list of accommodations along with personalities, quirks, age of old pubs and dogs. And: "Don't get lost in Stone'enge in the Druids circle, will yer." I loved the superstitious old maniac.

It was so dark I muffed all his instructions and caught a bleak grocery store economizing on its light bill. It was an old story: they must have liked blokes on bikes who come in out of a winter's night looking half dead. So a hundred yards down the road, new directions came out like a guidebook with colored illustrations. " . . . with the white walls and blue door," I got with repetitions.

This chap followed me out and down the street to make sure I had found it. As I hesitated slightly on the pedals, I heard footsteps quicken like a colt broken loose in the night. I rang the doorbell and the footsteps stopped dead and returned. He was satisfied.

Bed and breakfast, the biggest bargain in the British Isles. It hardly pays a cyclist to swing his bedroll and pup tent under a hedge, though I do it in summer for that is the time and no farmer ever raises an eyebrow or posts a sign to keep me out.

I suffer gently the endearments of the mum who inevitably answers the door. I am given evening tea, which is never charged for. My bike is bedded down. The fires are stoked for me. I am given the run of the whole house. I am licked by the faithful hound. My tired joints are cared for in a special bath that everybody doesn't get. The very personal nature of an English bath is evident from the toothbrushes in tumblers, damp embroidered face cloths. The hot water says, "That's enough," as it reaches navel level and shuts off with a "There now."

Any moment my mum will be there synchronized with my cool sprint—bathroom to hallway to stairs to bedroom. " 'Urry up and get right in," she says, brandishing a hot water bottle. "You'll probably be sweatin' in the night." I am hoping sweat will follow present condition. The room, warmed by electric light, is yet to know sweat. "The necessary is under the bed. Saves you walking all the way down to the bathroom past the dog."

Mum's with a message for the pilgrims of this world.

Hot water bottle kicked out during the night, landing in embossed earthenware receptacle. Made a mental note with those silly things that one thinks of in the night so that if ever I run a pub I could name it "Bird and Hottie."

The sausages and bacon and never-ending toast powered me through thirty miles of morning cycling into Wiltshire and there was Stonehenge coming up over a hump of Salisbury plains. You know how you expect the heavens to do something special, personal, at given times? So it was with murky morning undrizzled shafts of light coming right through onto the pile to show it was right there in its primitive and external setting.

But my pilgrimage was all but botched up at this stage. The National Trust, which looks after these monuments, had put in a big parking lot nearby, trying to save matters by lowering the ticket office cum cafeteria cum postcard stand cum toilet cum turnstile to ground level, placating the wrath of the purists with an underground tunnel, built under the guise of safety, to let them plod carless under the freeway to the other side — the pristine preserves of Stonehenge.

I was late with my message to the world. The postcards had beaten me to it and showed the midwinter sun in emphasized color doing strange tricks of light through narrow chinks in the big stones.

Fortunately there was no one to interfere and I went about my rites. I left my bike in the National Trust dugout. Taking a parcel from the carrier, I passed through the turnstile and the underground passage, which was Marineland-by-the-bay, and out onto the greensward, which was the real thing.

In the center of the inner circle of sarsens, or upright monoliths, I found a good sitting stone. It was one that might have plopped down after a couple of thousand years and like an iceberg just showed a fraction of its underground size. The rain had done a good job of rounding it out, plus a few centuries of graffiti.

"Please don't carve your name on these stones. They have been here for a long time," said a recent plaque, and I mentally completed the verse. "Your name will wash away in a millennium. And then you might be finally forgotten."

Not having leaf or pipe for a mind trip, I nevertheless came prepared. I had a bottle of cider in the cycle pack, a can of mentholated snuff in my pocket, and some notepaper.

After the warm rough taste of the powerful Devon cider, I took a pinch of snuff, first left nostril then right. The top of my head lifted pleasantly to a point on a level with the top of the lintels, or stone crosspieces. At this point of the blast I was able to observe the whole construction with clarity.

With clarity also I could see the reason for my pilgrimage. I could see the pitfalls. I could not yet see the outcome—it would have to wait. Exclamation points and obscenities excluded, I wrote this letter on the notepaper. Included are quotes from the only other persons present, a scholarly-looking guide who was conducting a young Pakistani student.

Dear Everyman,

If you are coming from California on one of those trips to "See Europe and Stonehenge by Globeshrinker," you may be making a mistake. You are a shrinkout, meaning you have shrunk the wrong thing. You will find the plane a poor vehicle. The time saved in it is loss of comprehension for one week. In that time you could have come by boat.

As boats are expensive, impatient, romantic things and are only thought about and planes always caught, please bring a bicycle.

Leaving London, take a train to Exeter. Cycle back to Stonehenge, taking a long time.

"Midsummer the sun rises on the heel stone striking through the circle. The axial line of the sun divides at right angles the burial set in the innermost ring." It first glances off the tops of hundreds of cars in the parking lot, picking up the long shadows of the candy wrappers and the heads poking from some steaming sleeping bags that the groundsman missed. The brown rays come shooting first through the smoke of a factory complex five miles away to be further diffused in the just cutoff exhausts of the proximate cars. You will see all miraculously lined up through the pillars and the craning necks of the mini-transported, Thermos-carrying, clucking tourists.

Astrologically alone this is a significant moment.

The position of the midwinter sun striking Stonehenge is rather hard to fix. If on bicycle, it will be almost impossible to get a reading due to the shakes. By lining up the chinks between the inner circle and the outer and an electricity pylon on the distant plain, it is possible to get a faint glimmer on the altar stone.

But please leave your ten new pence by the plastic, heated, amplified change window because after four thousand years they have suddenly decided that this place needs something for upkeep.

I would advise you, Everyman, to not make this a religious pilgrimage.

"It would be rash to infer that there was a religious outlook of the builders though it does betray some preoccupation with the sun. It's possible that we have here an expression of the idea that life proceeds from death, one that easily has been combined with fertility cults. Yet there is no need to read into the fact of orientation any more than that the builders of Stonehenge shared an interest in the solar calendar common to most people whose livelihood is in any degree bound up with husbandry." Get your own religious blast perhaps with the use of a little snuff and cider, walking around from the outer circle to the inner in ever-diminishing circles to lie wiped out on the slaughter stone.

"Ambrosius, king of the Britons, consulted Merlin as to how best to commemorate his nobles slain in battle by Hengist the Saxon and the king was bidden to fetch the Giant's Dance from Mount Killaurus in Ireland, a magic circle the stones of which would stand forever. The king defeated the Irish in battle, but not surprisingly his soldiers tried in vain to shift the stones. Only with the aid of Merlin's magic did they finally succeed in carrying them away across the sea and reerecting them in Stonehenge." Prostrate as you will certainly be by now, Everyman, from jet lag and overbicycling, do have a gander at the upper structures. Contemplate how they dragged the fifty-ton verticals from the Marlborough Downs, about twenty-five miles away. Then like the start of a house of cards they stacked the five-ton lintels across the top. The lintels came from the coast by no fast freight 150 miles away.

For your own benefit, take a look at the small doves smart enough to wait for a few centuries until some little crevices got washed away in the granite.

Then realize, Everyman friend, that it isn't all songs and chanting — nor cranes and bulldozers — but just those smart little guys who wait around and take their time who find the niche in the years.

Take your photos, grab a jet, and run. You've got the story.

"Although in general appearance Stonehenge may strike us as barbarous, the monument has been laid out with great precision. The lintels have been most carefully secured to their uprights by tenon and mortise, and to their neighbors by tongue-and-groove joints. The implements to carve these were stone, not metal . . . stone worked away at stone."

Much chastened,
   I am

            Yours sincerely,
               Peter Lawlor

2 History and Lore

Everyone knows that Henry Ford built the Model T and that Ralph Nader offed the Corvair. In between, lots happened but who cares? Only motor-crazy chrome freaks, and they deserve a mouthful of exhaust, not an historical treatise.

The time has come to create a new pantheon, to resuscitate past heroes and beg them lend mythic distinction to the bicycle renascence. Imagine a drum roll, a trumpet blare—out of the mist ride the forgotten ones. Giovanni Fontana, Chevalier de Sivrac, Baron Karl Von Drais, Kirkpatrick ("Daft Pate") MacMillan, a superpowered Justice League, they return now, here, at the tail end of the twentieth century to exercise their spirit will. Regard them well—upon their work, thou ride.

On July 20, 1962, Frenchman Jose Meiffret set a new bicycle speed record of 117.98 miles per hour. To make that record, the fifty-year-old pedaler rode behind a specially adapted racing car on which was mounted an elaborate windshield designed to give the rider a minute, but substantial, edge because of lowered wind resistance.

The twenty-four-hour distance record was set in Australia in 1932 by Hubert Opperman, who pedaled a distance of 860 miles, 367 yards. The one-hour distance record was set in 1928 by Belgium's Leon Vanderstuyft, who covered 76 miles, 504 yards in those sixty short minutes.

Man's first primitive impulses to bicycle are revealed in the sculptured bas-reliefs of a first century B.C. Middle Eastern Mervinian culture. In unmistakable detail, the relic shows a woman dressed as a warrior riding a two-wheel vehicle, holding onto a handlebar steering mechanism.

Centuries passed before Christianity evolved an equivalent symbol. It was not until 1580 at a little church in Stoke Poges, England, that the faithful could worship in the presence of a stained-glass cherub astride a wooden frame bicycle, kicking up its heels and trumpeting toward heaven.

The response to, Who invented the first bicycle? varies from country to country. As early as 1418, Giovanni Fontana of Padua, Italy, designed a small carriage powered by a circle of rope running through a pulley. The rider sat in the wagon and pulled the rope, thereby setting a system of gears in motion that made the wheels go round. More than three hundred years later in 1764, an Englishman named Ovendon was among many inventors working on man-operated carriages. His contribution was a carriage capable of traveling six miles per hour with ease and, with great exertion, up to ten miles per hour. Designed for the rich, this machine was meant to be powered by a footman who stood in the back and trod alternately on two pedal planks. While the servant labored, the master was to steer with a set of reins.

Chevalier de Sivrac designed and built the earliest two-wheeled, rider-powered vehicle in France in 1790. Named the Celefire, this machine had some distinct disadvantages. It had no brakes, it could not be steered, and since the wheels were joined by a rigid bar, it could scarcely corner. Despite being painted to resemble either a boa constrictor or a lion, and offering the option of a padded saddle, the Celefire failed to catch the public's fancy.

A toy more to the liking of the masses was produced in 1816 by Baron Karl Von Drais in Karlsruhe, Germany. Called a Draisine, the baron's creation was described as a comfortable two-wheeled vehicle consisting of a wooden bar, with a saddle, attached to two medium-sized wheels that the rider propelled by pushing his feet backward against the ground. It was steered by a handle attached to the front axle. This vehicle, though it weighed anywhere from forty to sixty pounds, caught on famously in England. It became known as the hobbyhorse or dandyhorse and soon attained fad status among fashionable young men who even attended special schools to learn how to ride. The craze lasted four or five years.

Being susceptible to termites and dry rot, and hard to push uphill, the hobbyhorse was soon replaced by a sturdier mechanism. It remained for a Scottish blacksmith, who pulled people's teeth in his spare time, to successfully work out the mechanics of pedal power. In 1839, Kirkpatrick MacMillan, known as "Daft Pate" to neighbors who looked warily on the curious contraption he invented and rode, developed a full-fledged wooden bicycle complete with a saddle and rear-wheel drive.

Another two and one-half years passed before Daft Pate made his first historic long distance ride. After three years of experimentation, he set out on June 6, 1842, on a journey from his hometown of Penpoint to visit his three brothers in Glasgow. Destined to achieve many firsts, he earned the distinction during this jaunt of having the world's first bicycle accident. In a careless moment, he knocked down a child and the very next day was fined five shillings for "riding to the danger of the public."

Until October, 1851, MacMillan reigned as the undisputed inventor of the bicycle. Then, from the distant regions of the Soviet Union, came a claim that a peasant from the Penza province, known only as Artamonov, rode a bicycle of his own invention into Moscow in 1801. The news report said that Artamonov was given his idea by other Russians who built three- and four-wheeled vehicles as far back as 1752.

Almost two decades elapsed before Parisians Pierre and Ernest Michaux introduced a bicycle with a rotating crank integral with the front hub (an idea "adapted from the handle of a grindstone," wrote Ernest in 1893). The Michaux machine was called a velocipede in formal language and a boneshaker in slang, because of the rough ride the iron-rimmed wooden wheels provided when bumping over cobblestones.

The 1860s were a time of advance. Solid rubber tires were affixed to the boneshaker in 1869, as was a chain-drive mechanism. But the real great leap forward was the first bicycle factory, a brainchild of the entrepreneurial Michaux brothers. By 1865, their factory was turning out four hundred bicycles a year. As fortune would have it, one of their mechanics, Pierre Lallement, designed a much better machine and, seeing little point in sticking around where the competition was already established, emigrated to the United States. He and a partner, James Carrol of Ansonia, Connecticut, took out the first American l ike patent.

Meanwhile, capitalism being what it is, the Michaux brothers jumped into mass production. They bought a sewing machine factory in Coventry, England — where labor was probably cheaper — and began cranking out bicycles for the French army just before the Franco-Prussian war. When the war started, the French army canceled its order. Unperturbed, the brothers solved their problem of several hundred surplus cycles by marketing the units at home. Thus Coventry became the birthplace of the British cycle industry and was later to reach an output of more than two million cycles per year.

In 1870, James Starley, foreman and one of the founders of the Coventry factory, patented a tension-spoked wheel for sewing machines in which the rim and the hub were connected by looped wire spokes. Still in full possession of his wits at age sixty-seven, he saw the possibilities for other applications and in the same year designed a light bicycle with a large driving front wheel and a smaller rear wheel. Based on the ordinary or penny-farthing model invented the year before in Paris, the new model, christened the Ariel, offered several improvements: it was the first all-metal bike; double wire spokes could be adjusted to make the wheel more or less rigid; it had a mounting step so that cyclists were no longer obliged to take a running leap and a vault into the saddle; by pulling a cord attached to the handlebars, the rear wheel could be braked; but most important of all, it was considerably lighter than any other bicycle.

Starley's improved Ariel made bicycling a means of transportation, a popular pastime, and a sport. Allegedly, part of the appeal of the Ariel was that it was extremely tricky to control. Skill and daring went into maneuvering it and many a bruise, broken bone, and an occasional death, came to those who weren't total masters of the machines.

Out of some purist impulse, original cycling enthusiasts resisted attempts to improve the bicycle, both in its mechanics and in its safety devices. They felt a rapport with the Ariel and had little but disdain for a more predictable vehicle. The first innovation to be stayed by their wrath was the chain drive, invented in 1879 by one H. J. Lawson. Little is known about Lawson except that he received a gold watch from the cycling industry for his efforts. The first model to feature his improvement was snidely labeled the Crocodile by the hordes of loyal Arielists who refused to have anything to do with a more efficient newcomer.

The first design to break the impasse was the American Star of 1880. Previous high-wheeler design forced the rider to sit directly on top of the front wheel. If the bike swerved or stuck, his momentum would carry him headfirst over the handlebars, a patently dangerous state of affairs. The American Star reversed the position of the wheels by putting the large drive wheel to 'the rear and the small balance wheel to the front. Though people fell off just as often, they now fell on their backs, hence satisfying both thrill-seeking purists and those of a more efficacious turn of mind.

The purists' rule was short-lived, however, for in five years, bicycles began to evolve rapidly toward their present form. In 1885, the best and most successful alteration of the machine — an alteration that has survived to this day — was put into production by John K. Starley, nephew of the Coventry sewing machine factory Starley. His model featured the diamond-style frame, invented in 1869, and the infamous rear chain drive. By 1888, a Belfast veterinary surgeon, John Boyd Dunlop, adapted the pneumatic tire to the bicycle. Though this development also encountered great resistance, racing proved the worth of these new tires.

In 1890, the Broncho Light Roadster shattered convention by making both wheels the same size, though the pedals were still attached to the rear axle with the rider seated directly over them. The wheels, however, were set too close together on this model, making it difficult to manage and likely to tip over backward. By 1893, high-wheel bicycles were a thing of the past. The inimitable Starleys brought all innovations together in one machine, the Rover Safety. It featured a lowered diamond frame with the seat set over the mid-frame pedals, which drove wheels of equal diameter. The Starley Rover also offered direct steering, coasters, and a brake. While it was initially christened the Beetle by sporting types, its quality won out and it remains the dominant style of bicycle to this day.

One of the more interesting aspects of any invention is the social changes it brings and the aberrations it spawns. For some, bicycles presented a moral dilemma that began with a vague concern that perhaps it was not right for mere mortal men to travel so fast. The Moscow Society of Velocipede Lovers gave the renowned Count Leo Tolstoy, sixty-seven, a bicycle and an instructor free of charge. A neighbor, upon seeing the bearded rider glide past his door, chided: "Tolstoy has learned to ride a bicycle. Is this not inconsistent with his Christian ideals?" After reflecting deeply on the matter, the gray-haired sage disavowed his indulgence and became a good walking Christian again. Sigmund Freud so hated bicycles that once, while hunting for a vacation spot, he wrote a letter home stating that Mondsee was not acceptable because of the number of cyclists on the main road. He went so far as to urge that everyone campaign against bicycles because they raised so much dust and knocked down great numbers of children.

A more widespread problem existed for women. Bicycling rose to prominence during the Victorian period, a period which confined women to wearing long, full skirts that got caught in the wheels. Altering skirts proved too daring an alternative, so the efforts of Victorian designers went into altering bicycles.

Cycling was denounced from many a pulpit as a pastime comparable to drinking and gambling. A group of liberated young women in Cape May, New Jersey, a resort town, began pedaling around with corsets and caused no end of talk among the elderly and the censorious. In reaction, the Cape May Anti-Bicycle Club was formed, and futilely tried to stem the rising tide of bike freaks. Its one small victory was a Cape May law passed in 1896 limiting bicycle speed to eight miles per hour. In the mid-1890s, antifun forces mustered a number of doctors who began warning of the dire results that might be brought about by the new mode of transportation. They maintained that "schorchers" were apt to go more rapidly to the grave than "victims of galloping consumption" and, moreover, many probably would be candidates for mental institutions as well. A physician then serving on California's insanity commission double-talked his way out of coming to grips with the issue, leaving for posterity this empty aphorism: "It is not the use but the abuse of what may aid us that is to be feared."

The period's emphasis on modesty had gone as far as it could without covering women in bags. Ladies in the 1880s did not show their ankles in public unless they were some kind of hussy. Working hard to preserve decency, one bike firm developed a "bat-wing" shield, which folded back between the wheels and hid the entire pedal mechanism, legs included. In 1886, an E. G. Latta took out a patent for drop-frame bicycles, much like the diamond frame with the top bar missing. This allowed skirts to remain full and hanging, and obviated the danger of exposing flesh. Two years later, a Mr. Smith of Washington, so the story goes, created a public stir when he persuaded his wife to ride one such bike down Pennsylvania Avenue. Mrs. Smith, escorted by several male chaperons, all relatives, is alleged to be the first woman to ride a safety bicycle in public.

Practicality has a way of outing, however, and some time around 1890, the bloomer became acceptable dress for women. The style had been developed some forty years previous but never caught on until the advent of the bicycle. Cycling soon lost most of its male chauvinist aura and became a true people's pastime.

In a more serious vein, bicycles have brought new opportunities for crime: theft, which comes as no surprise, and certain forms of extortion. In 1933, a racket group known as "The Bloody Bicyclists" preyed on unsuspecting motorists in New York's Central Park. Young men, all prepared with torn trousers, bloodstained shirts, and scratched and gory legs, worked in relays riding their bikes in front of automobiles and then crashing into a wall or fence. The "victim" then screamed at the motorist "working" him, denounced him as a hit-and-run driver, and asked him to pay from $10 to $25 to avoid being reported to the police.

Bicycle thieves seem generally to be a boring lot, but in 1956, one eleven-year-old Daly City, California, youth distinguished himself with his Robin Hood temperament. According to police, the lad gave away fifteen bicycles, all of which he had stolen. And he was even brassy enough to report a similar theft to the police when a bicycle was stolen from him. He had, of course, originally stolen the purloined machine.

As is the case in every evolutionary process, certain bicycle mutations have occurred. On land, on sea, and in the air, the basic mechanism has been adapted to a wide variety of vehicles. And tinkering with the bike has inspired other inventors to greater works yet.

Water cycles were the first such mutation to appear, reaching their heyday in the 1890s. In that decade, a triplet water cycle ridden by former racing cyclist F. Cooper and two companions covered 101 miles of the river Thames, from Putney to Oxford, in 19 hours, 27 minutes, 50 seconds. This bested the efforts of a triple-sculls boat teamed by good university oarsmen who covered the same course in 22 hours, 28 seconds, approximately an 18 percent advantage for the machine. While the date has been lost, a team of six women reached a speed of fifteen miles per hour on the Seine. And on April 17, 1929, Roger Vincent of Paris made a crossing of the English Channel, pedaling from Calais to Dover, in 5 hours, 35 minutes. This was Vincent's first venture on the sea. He had previously confined himself to the placid Seine.

Air cycles have never shown the success characteristic of their water brethren. The first air cycle trials were held in France at the turn of the century at the Parisian Parc des Princes. An observer, G. H. Stancer, wrote that the 199 entrants only accomplished short "jumps." In Germany in the 1930s, an air cycle flew two hundred yards. But then development of air cycles went into a slump until the 1960s when a British industrialist, Henry Kramer, made a standing offer of £5,000 to go to the first flier to complete a figure eight over a distance of one mile.

In 1961, spurred by the lure of easy money, the Puffin Mark 1, developed by the Hatfield Manpowered Aircraft Club and piloted by John Wimpenny, flew fifty yards, at five feet off the ground. The very next year, an improved model went way past the previous record – about one-half a mile – in two minutes. Neither machine could attempt the turns required by the prize conditions.

So much for the sea and the air. It is on land that monstrosities have flourished. During the 1890s, a bicycle built for ten was made by the Waltham Manufacturing Company. Also during the decade, there appeared a one and one-half ton tricycle, with two eleven-foot and one six-foot wheels, requiring eight men to operate it. In its first test, from Boston to Concord, New Hampshire, it covered 150 miles. In 1969, Steve McPeach, then a senior at Seattle Pacific College, was frequently seen riding a twenty-foot-high unicycle about town. McPeach acknowledged that his greatest fear was that he might fall off backward from the machine and said he even had nightmares about the possibility.

Another mutant was the battle bike, a small fifteen-pound machine that folded up so the rider could carry it over terrain unsuited for wheeled vehicles. These folding bikes first went to war during the Boer War in 1899. The soldier in that day could ride to battle, his rifle attached to his front wheel. Once near the line, all he had to do was twist the bike here and there, put it on his back, and truck off into combat.

The grand anomaly of bicycle experiments came in the 1960s when a chemist, David E. H. Jones, noticed that a moving bicycle without a rider can travel as long as twenty seconds without falling over. The stability attracted his attention and in an effort to discover its cause he tried to mechanically counteract it. His goal was an unridable bicycle.

His first suspicion was that gyroscopic forces, those generated by spin, of the front wheel kept everything in balance. So Jones built the Unridable Bicycle Mark I, a bike normal in every way except for an extra front wheel mounted off the ground in such a manner as to be able to counterrotate and generate opposing gyroscopic forces, which would cancel out those produced by the normal front wheel. The experiment was doomed to failure, as no matter which way the extra wheel was spun, the machine proved ridable.

Undaunted, Jones began to test the hypothesis that steering geometry creates stability. According to this idea, what counts is the location of the point at which the front wheel touches the ground with respect to the steering axis. The steering axis is a line running down the steering post to the ground. If stability is a function determined by a function of whether the contact point is in front of the steering axis or behind it, a wheel directly under the steering axis should be highly unstable.

Or so Jones thought. Unridable Bicycle Mark II was fitted with such a wheel, an adapted furniture castor. The results were extremely inconclusive because the machine's evident unstability was not caused by a counteracting of forces but could be attributed to the fact that the castor could not ride over a bump higher than half an inch. The castor also became extremely hot when the bike was pedaled at any speed.

Unridable Bicycle Mark III tackled the steering geometry problem in a new way. Its front fork was bent backward toward the rider, instead of forward as is usual. Jones foolishly expected Mark III to be highly unstable, but to his surprise the machine could run for many yards without a rider. Any difficulty to the ride was caused by the *improved* stability interfering with the rider's normal reflexes.

There are times in most people's lives that to reach their goals they feel they must call on a power greater than their own. So it was with Jones. With the aid of a program called Bicyc, he sought to analyze the source of Mark III's stability with a computer.

Jones learned that the farther the contact point is moved behind the steering axis, the stronger is the torque, or twisting force, exerted on the axis when the bicycle leans over. The torque stabilizes the bicycle by turning the wheel in the direction of the lean. Another force, the castering force, prevents oversteering by causing the rest of the bicycle to swing into line behind the turning front wheel.

In order to confirm the importance of these forces, the unrelenting Jones built Unridable Bicycle Mark IV. Whereas the front-wheel contact point of Mark III was behind the steering axis, the front wheel of Mark IV was mounted four inches ahead of its normal position, so that its contact point was well forward of the steering axis. Success comes to those who persevere. This contraption reversed the effect of lean-induced torque. The Unridable Bicycle Mark IV was exceptionally hard to ride and crashed instantly when released while moving without a rider. The commercial possibility of this invention has yet to be explored, but if wealthy ranch owners in this country can be paid to not grow food while numerous people in the world starve, it is not unreasonable to assume that there may one day be a place for the Unridable Bicycle in our economy.

Little record was left of the battle bike's worth in the Boer

War. During World War II, however, it initially proved useful
to the Japanese. On the morning of December 8, 1941, exactly
when Pearl Harbor was being attacked (if one takes into account the International Datelines), the Japanese had twenty
troopships, with an escort of destroyers, threatening Malaya
with three infantry divisions, four tank regiments, several
artillery units, and twenty thousand bicycles. The entire task
force numbered sixty thousand men. The British, who had been
blocking Japanese seaports at the time (a point U.S. history
does not draw much attention to), had the advantage of prepared positions and superior numbers, but the Japanese had
better air support and greater mobility. The mobility came
from the bicycles.

By the time Malaya was attacked, Japan controlled most of
China and Indochina. The attraction of Malaya was that that
country then produced nearly one-half of the world's rubber
and one-third of its tin. Although the planning for the campaign had been hurried, it was still thorough. Each of the three
infantry divisions got a special issue of six hundred trucks and
six thousand bicycles. In the field, the soldier could carry all
his equipment on the machine. With his rifle over his shoulder,
his light machine gun on the handlebar, and his backpack, he
had a load of almost one hundred pounds. Each company also
transported a small mobile repair shop.

The Japanese strategy was to let the infantry force the British into retreat and then send in the bicycle brigades to harass
and dog the English, never giving them opportunity to regroup,
always keeping them under pressure. In combat, the bicycle
troops would leave their bicycles under guard and behind the
lines. After the skirmish, they would retrieve the machines
and take up the chase. River crossings, which delayed trucks
for days, were no obstacle to the cyclists who waded across
holding their machines aloft.

The British, on the other hand, were fighting massive traffic
jams in addition to the Japanese. In the final battle, which took
place on Singapore Island, the land-bicycle strategy proved to
be a decisive factor. For years, Singapore had been an impreg-
nable fortress—from attack by the sea. No strategist had an-
ticipated that an enemy might approach by land. Monstrous

guns were pointed the wrong way and could not be turned around. Just seventy days after the Japanese had landed, General Percival surrendered. In those seventy days, the Japanese had advanced sixty thousand men through terrain that would have been exceedingly hostile to motorized transport. The edge that helped secure this victory was the bicycle.

The first recorded bicycle race, unofficial and a challenge match only, was instigated by none other than the inventor of the first ridable bicycle himself, the Scotsman Kirkpatrick MacMillan. On that historic first ride to see his brothers, fresh from claiming simultaneous credit for the first accident and the first accident involving a child, he bet a coachman friend working on the Glasgow-Carlisle line that he could beat the coach to the town of Sanquhar. Racing conditions were hardly equitable since the bicycle did not have to stop for mail and passengers. But being either obviously short on brains or rashly contemptuous of the new invention, the coachman accepted. The race went neck and neck but as of the first stop MacMillan pulled ahead and easily bested his friendly competitor.

By the 1860s, Pierre and Ernest Michaux were producing their velocipedes or boneshakers. On May 31, 1868, Napoleon III offered a gold medal for a cycle race and James Moore, an Englishman then living in Paris, was the winning contestant and a declared French champion. This Moore was to prove a savior as far as the French were concerned, when one year later he took first prize in the first official competitive race.

The race attracted an international response to a challenge issued by a fortnightly paper devoted to the new pastime, called *Le Vélocipède Illustré*. The event was conceived by Paul Ruinert, and organized by Richard Lesclide, personal secretary to Victor Hugo. A total of 305 contestants registered for the race. They were divided into evens and odds for the purpose of having one group leave a half hour later than the other from the starting point opposite the Arc de Triomphe, Avenue de la Grande Armée. The route, which took the racers through Saint-Germain, Mantes, Vernon, and Louviers to Rouen, was a distance of 123 kilometers or 76 miles.

James Moore was in the second group to leave and was reportedly incensed by the delay. He vowed to make up the half hour and be the first across the finish line. True to his word, he pedaled like a man possessed. By the time he reached Saint-Germain he had left the others behind and was catching up with the stragglers from the first group. Moore, who was something of a folk hero, pedaled standing up. At the time, his style was considered dashing, and he drew cheers and encouragement from spectators. Still, Moore was not the only cyclist from the second group that was making good time. One noteworthy fellow was Pierre Bellay, of the Lyons Veloce Club, who was riding a monster tricycle weighing seventy pounds.

Shortly after Monte, bicycles began breaking down and Moore drew aside the leader of the first group, Count A. de Castera. The count, realizing that Moore had closed a half hour gap, offered to pace Moore to the finish. Politely refusing the offer because of the possibility of a rally on the part of other contestants, Moore pulled ahead, all alone and in the lead, and several hours later arrived in Rouen having completed the seventy-six miles in 10 hours, 45 minutes, an average of just over seven miles per hour. His reward was a medal, a diary, and a thousand-franc note, a yearly wage for a gentleman at that time.

There followed many such events. Championship races on the high bicycle were established in 1878 when the National Cyclists' Union, formerly the Bicycle Union, was founded in England and the universities of Cambridge and Oxford recognized the new sport. The Ordinary championships, named after a style of bike, continued until 1892. In 1882, the first bicycle superstar, H. L. Cortis, won all national titles for one-, five-, twenty-five-, and fifty-mile races. In that same year, also on an ordinary, he was the first man to ride more than twenty miles an hour on the same style machine. Title racing in the United States began in 1883 and G. M. Hendrie won a challenge cup from W. G. Rowe and became America's first bicycling champion.

It was not until the 1890s, known in pedalers' circles as the Golden Age of bicycling, that racing became prominent. Since then cycling has been a major organized sport, with championship events in two main categories: road racing and track racing. Internationally, the sport is governed by the Union Cycliste Internationale (UCI), formed in 1900 with Belgium, France, Switzerland, and the United States as charter members. The UCI sets rules and standards for participation, verifies speed records, and controls both professional and amateur events. Currently more than seventy countries are members of the UCI.

The first "character" to emerge from American racing was the phenomenal A. A. Zimmerman, who pedaled as small a gear as was then possible on the highwheeler and won his races through his unbelievable ability to spin the pedals around at high speed. In 1899, Charles M. ("Mile-a-Minute") Murphy caused a sensation when he rode on a wooden track behind a train carrying a windshield, in an effort to break the one-minute bicycle mile. His first attempt failed when the train proved too slow. Murphy had to slow down to avoid running into it from the rear. The second attempt was successful but ended with a minor disaster. Murphy completed the mile in fifty-four and four-fifths seconds but the engine driver shut down the steam too soon. Quick-thinking helpers on the end of the Pullman caught Murphy and pulled him on board just as his bicycle rammed the train.

And out of the 1890s rode Major Taylor, an American black man who dominated the world racing scene from the turn of the century until shortly before World War I. Taylor, who won his first race at age thirteen, beat the fastest riders on three continents. Three of his records are still on the books: the one-quarter, three-quarters, and one mile human-paced mark. One of his inventions continues to be optional equipment on fine bicycles. This is an adjustable handlebar on some racing machines that permits the handlebar to be moved forward or backward into the position that best suits the rider. This is known as a Major Taylor Outrigger.

Taylor was one of eight children whose father was a coachman for a wealthy Indianapolis family. He was born on November 26, 1878, and christened Marshall W. Taylor. In his earliest teens, he was employed in a cycle shop. The shop's owner annually sponsored a ten-mile road race that attracted some of Indiana's finest riders, lured by the first-prize gold medal. At his employer's urging, Taylor entered the race and

won by a margin of a mere six seconds. In admiration, a towns-
man nicknamed him Major, and he used the sobriquet thereafter as his formal name. By the time he had reached sixteen,
Taylor had raced all over the Midwest with a high win record.
He was employed primarily as an instructor and coach by a
retired racer turned manufacturer named L. D. Munger.

Taylor's prowess stemmed from a fine combination of brawn,
coordination, and strategy. He worked out with light dumb-
bells, Indian clubs, and pulley weights, and maintained his
exercise schedule even when traveling. He followed a strict
diet and never smoked or drank. He was also a deeply pious
man of strong convictions who refused to race on Sundays. His
movements were allegedly smooth and beautiful to behold.
After his third European tour, two French journalists wrote:

"It has been said that he has the form of a marquise, and
when in action, the feline gait of a black panther, watching the
moving jungle of bicycles. At times he creeps and is ready to
spring, then he jumps, the final dazzling sprint where the rider
goes straight as lightning with no visible effort, and without
the slightest twist of his blue jersey, motionless on the whirl-
wind of black feet which turn faster and faster until he has
won."

On the track, Taylor was watchful and thinking all the
time. In one of his races with Tom Cooper, he counted pedal
revolutions and calculated that his opponent was riding a gear
of 108 teeth as compared to his own of 92. Further, he deduced
Cooper was using extralength cranks as well. Anticipating the
other rider's plan of action, he adjusted his own accordingly
and easily won.

Tom Cooper was a close friend to another prominent bicycling figure, Barney Oldfield. Born in the late 1870s, his first
work out with a bicycle came at age fifteen. He was then serving as a bellhop in a hotel and noticed that one guest stored a
lightweight Cleveland bicycle in the basement. It was an easy
matter for Oldfield to appropriate the bike each evening and
return it each morning after a hard night of fast riding around
the deserted streets of his hometown, Toledo, Ohio.

Oldfield, like many riders, was attracted to the sport by its
prize money. At sixteen, he entered Toledo's Decoration Day

races and won the first prize, a diamond ring. He entered the Ohio State Championship Races in the spring of 1895 and won two silver medals and a gold watch. The victory caught the attention of the Stearns Bicycle Company, and shortly thereafter it hired Oldfield as a salesman and racer of its machines. As his tours extended from Ohio to other parts of the country, he became known as a particularly aggressive rider.

Oldfield's ability to mix it up was his prime virtue. He adapted easily to the custom of elbowing and handlebar locking, which lead racers used on anyone who threatened to pass them. He enjoyed spectacular upsets and had few illusions about what fans wanted. "They pay money to see me risk my neck, and I need their money. I might as well be dead as dead broke."

His cycling career lasted for six years until Tom Cooper persuaded him to end it. Both had agreed that working in factories in the winter and racing in the good weather year after year wasn't getting them too far. The two parted company for a while. Tom went to Detroit where he met a young mechanic named Henry Ford, who was building racing cars. Cooper dashed off a letter to Oldfield and the rest is no longer bicycle lore. Barney, who once referred to automobiles as "bedframes on wheels" and vowed that he wouldn't be caught dead in one of them, became, in the early twentieth century, the epitome of the daredevil automobile racer.

It wasn't just people who gained reputations in bicycling— certain places and events were notorious too. During the 1900s, the place to be was in Salt Lake City, Utah, at the Salt Palace, an enormous race track, which was part of an amusement complex that included a bowery with large lawns and flower beds, a dance hall, theater, and beer garden. Built in 1903 by a syndicate of local businessmen, the complex was destroyed by fire ten years later and was never reconstructed.

But in its heyday all the great names in bicycle racing appeared at the track: Ivor and Gussie Lawson, Hardy Downing, Fred Whittler, W. E. Samuelson, and many others. The arena drew competitors from three continents for the Salt Palace races, which ran Wednesday and Saturday nights from Memorial Day to Labor Day.

The track was eight laps to the mile with a forty-eight-degree bank, and was constructed out of wood like the hull of a ship. Flood lights were spaced about every thirty feet so that there was ample illumination for night riding. Races varied in length from sprints of one-half mile to two miles with occasional races of several miles, which were run by pairs of riders who spelled each other off. One of the most popular races was the Australian pursuit race, which called for four men to be spaced equidistant around the track. At the starting gun, each rider tried to overtake the man in front of him, who then had to drop out of the race, until there was one rider left. There were the usual handicaps, relays, and special lap races, but the super crowd pleaser was motor-paced racing.

In motor-paced racing, each rider followed behind a motorcycle that carried a windbreak. A roller, much like a modern paint roller made out of wood, extended a few inches beyond the rear wheel of the motorcycle so that if the bike rider came too close he would hit the roller, making it spin furiously but otherwise causing no damage to the bike or the rider. The pedalists made a practice of riding close because the motorcycle riders would stuff newspapers or cardboard around their legs to create a vacuum that would help pull the bike along. If a rider dropped back more than a foot or so behind the motorcycle, he would lose the advantage of the vacuum. With the noise of the motors, the rumble of the windbreaks, and the proximity of bike and motorcycle, spectator excitement would quickly accelerate.

The competitors pedaled under a contract of $1,800 to $2,000 for the Salt Palace's three-month season, with the contract specifying bonuses of $35 for a win, $25 for a second, and $15 for a third. They raced as often as management wanted them to. The daredevil of the palace was Hardy K. Downing, who performed a loop-the-loop act in circuses and carnivals when he wasn't racing. He rode his bike down a steep track about thirty feet off the ground and then around a vertical circle nine or ten feet in diameter — a sensational trick that depended on a lot of momentum. Downing, when his bike days were over, became Utah's most successful boxing promoter, giving Jack Dempsey his first professional fight for a purse of $5. But throughout his life he continued to regard bicycling as the greatest participation and spectator sport in the world. "It had the speed, danger, and thrills to lure the crowds," he said shortly before his death. "Somebody should have saved it, and given a chance, it will come back."

A harsher form of competition briefly sprang up during the thirties and died shortly thereafter under the weight of public pressure. For 1930 was the summer of the marathon epidemic. Shipwreck Kelly set a new flagpole-sitting record atop the Steel Pier in Atlantic City and set off the rage. There were contests in chair rocking, kite flying, boat rowing, baseball pitching, seesawing, and sitting on corners, and, as fate would have it, bicycling. The rules varied from team to team. A group in New York allowed only two men on a team and no stopping whatsoever, while a New Jersey group had four riders and considered twenty-minute stops to be fair. Although some teams rode over a closed course, others found it more interesting to ride around the town and visit as they went along.

The trial often turned out to be greater than that of a mere ride. A New Jersey stalwart rode through a tornado that was destroying houses and barns around him. Another New Jersey fellow was almost literally knocked out of a race when an unidentified rival leaped from some bushes and bounced a baseball off his head. By August, both public and municipal interest had waned. That month, four cyclists and their manager were convicted of incorrigibility, and their parents were found guilty of negligence. The judge pronounced that the contests "have the effect of undermining the health of the children participating." Eventually official pressure ended the competition and the final record of some 880 hours went largely unnoticed by a then apathetic public.

A lighter aspect of group bicycling activities is touring, a practice established almost as soon as the cycle appeared. The Pickwick Bicycle Club in London was founded in 1870 and is the oldest in the world. This was quickly followed by the Cyclists' Touring Club, which organized in 1878 and had members scattered throughout Europe and North America.

These associations established the practice of publishing roadbooks, maps, and journals for travelers. They also recommended hotels, especially those with fixed rates so the unwary stranger wasn't fleeced, and appointed representatives to aid members who were on the road. They succeeded in inducing most governments to allow members to travel freely across frontiers without paying duty on their machines and worked diligently — and were taxed with equal diligence — for the improvement of roads.

In the United States, the granddaddy of touring clubs was the League of American Wheelmen, organized in 1880 with the objective of promoting bicycling for people of all ages, encouraging legislation favorable to cyclists, and planning and conducting cycling programs. Like its British counterpart, the league formed a touring bureau that received travel information from its many members and redistributed it in the form of roadbooks.

The league's earliest activities included actively championing the cause of bicycling against an often hostile business-government establishment. In 1879, the New York Board of Commissioners passed an ordinance excluding pedalers from Central Park. The LAW struggle to liberate the park for the people went on for a full eight years, ending with the "Liberty Bill," signed by the governor in 1887, revoking all laws discriminating against bicycles and the right of the people to tour on any street or highway in the state.

The league's growth was nothing short of phenomenal. So was its demise. One decade after its inception, it enjoyed a membership of 18,000 active pedalers. Three years later, the figure had jumped to 40,000 and by 1898, membership reached a maximum of 102,636. The roster included many later-to-be famous names such as Orville and Wilbur Wright, Commodore Cornelius Vanderbilt, and James ("Diamond Jim") Brady.

But with the advent of the horseless carriage, which today rules the roadways and soils the air, defection became the order of the day. By 1902, the league's ranks diminished to a mere 8,629 loyal riders. Thirty years later, there remained a meager 100 and it was only through the committed efforts of H. P. ("Jack") Hansen, a Chicago bicycle distributor and racer, that the organization continued to exist at all.

Fortune may ride with the league, however, for with the

current wave of renewed cycling enthusiasm, the league's purpose has been redefined and there is widespread interest in its aims and offerings. It now boasts a thriving active membership and has chapters in all fifty states, Canada, and several foreign countries.

And with contemporary ecological consciousness, there is certain to be greater loyalty to two-wheeled transport than was displayed by the faint of heart at the turn of the century.

3 Buying a Bicycle

So you wanna buy a bike? Well, just hop on down to your local shop, drop your coin on the counter, pick out a shiny, new model, and ride on! Right?

Wrong. Choosing the right bike is like choosing the right mate. Or the right analogy. A complex process at best.

Yet, after some experimentation and a little bit of theorizing, we've constructed (from nothing, mind you) a few basic guidelines that should help to simplify matters. With this concise guide in hand, you'll be able to avoid most common pitfalls. It's the uncommon ones that'll get you every time.

Buying a bicycle is like being lost in the woods on a rainy day and remembering your compass is in the raincoat you left hanging over the kitchen chair. A guide with an umbrella, this chapter leads the wandering buyer down the soggy trail of information to find the bicycle best for him.

There are five active ingredients in bicycle selection: (1) the bike's quality, (2) the bike's use, (3) the bike's cost, (4) the buyer's physical size and condition, and (5) the buyer's personal taste. Of the five, two stand out. The first is the most followed and most sought: quality. Measurable and tangible, a bicycle's quality comes from the realities of craftsmanship, precision, strength, resiliency, efficiency, weight, and cost. The second is the most ridiculous and most inconsistent: taste. Vague and sometimes strange, the buyer's taste comes straight from his mouth, and has little to do with the real world, for it savors the rich sauces of the ego and imagination.

To find the quality of a bicycle look at its parts.

Brakes

Generally, two brake designs are used on bicycles. Lower-priced, lower-quality bikes employ a side-pull brake — imprecise because one side of it applies pressure sooner and longer than the other side. (See figure 20.) Higher-quality bikes use center-pull brakes—a type that applies pressure from both sides equally, at the same time, and for the same length of time. (See figure 21.) Mafac is a good brand, as are Campagnolo, Weinmann, and Universal.

Cranks

High-performance ten-speeds are fitted with an easily removable aluminum crank, a design called cotterless. (See figure 18.) Lower-quality bikes use a heavier steel crank connected to a crank axle by a soft metal bolt. (See figure 16.) This cottered design makes repairs difficult because removing the cotter bolt is tricky. (See figure 17.) Buying a quality machine is buying a machine easy to work on. Cranks to look for are Campagnolo, Stronglight, T.A., and a fifth-grade teacher.

Rims and Tires

Rims and tires play a decisive role in a bicycle's maneuverability and resiliency. Quality bikes use a flexible aluminum rim that holds a lightweight tire called a sew-up because the tire casing is sewed around the inner tube. (See figure 41.) Lower-priced bikes employ heavier, rigid steel rims and conventional clincher tires. Separate from its inner tube, this tire clinches a lipped rim. (See figure 40.) The sew-up is held onto its rim by the tire's high pressure and special rim glue made by Clement and Tubasti. There is disagreement over the advantages and disadvantages of sew-up and clincher tires:

CLINCHER	SEW-UP
Advantages	*Advantages*
Available in all bike shops	Easier to change
Less expensive	More maneuverable
Easier to repair	Lightweight
Stronger—resistant to puncture	Compact when folded
	"Fast" for racing

Disadvantages	*Disadvantages*
Harder to change	More expensive
"Slow"	Harder to find
Heavier	Harder to repair
Bulky when folded	Easy to puncture

Rim types to look for are made by Mavic, Fiamme, and Wienmann.

Hubs

Hubs, like rims and tires, play an important role in determining the bicycle's lightness and maneuverability. On a precision bike, hubs are one piece of aluminum with hollow axles through which runs a quick-release rod that locks the wheel into the frame fork and permits the wheel to be removed quickly without tools. (See figure 36.) On lower-cost bikes, hubs are bolted into the fork and removal is accomplished only by using tools that are heavy to carry, hard to use, and easy to lose. Hub brands to look for are Campagnolo, Normandy, Cinelli, and Simplex.

Handlebars

Two handlebar styles are used on bicycles: flat and dropped. The dropped style is found on better-designed cycles and gives (1) a more effective and healthier riding position, (2) a method of allowing your arms, instead of your butt, to absorb the shock of rough roads, (3) an even distribution of body weight, and (4) five different hand positions helpful in combating weariness on long rides. (See figure 1.)

Derailleur (Gear-Changer)

The brains of the whole operation, the derailleur, is the bicycle's transmission, a simply designed but intricately built system of springs, cables, and small wheels that lifts the moving chain from one gear to another. (See figures 2 and 25.) There are two types of gear-changer: the internal three-speed

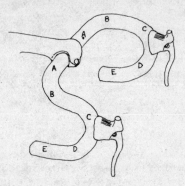

Fig. 1. Dropped handlebars showing the five hand positions that make riding easier. In the letter A position, the rider grasps the bar palms down with thumbs behind the bar and the back of the hand facing forward. In position B, the palms are on the bar's bend, the back of the hand facing "outward" (to the rider's left and right) and the thumbs on the inside of the bend. In C, the crotch between thumb and forefinger rests on the brake lever with thumbs to the inside. In the D position, the rider holds the bar at its bend just below the brake levers, thumbs turned inside and the hand's back facing outward. Position E is the same as D except it is held at the bottom of the bar.

Of the five positions, A and B are the most comfortable, C the most commonly used, and D and E the most efficient.

hub found, believe it or not, on three-speed cycles, and the more precision ten-speed derailleur (French for "derail"). Actually, ten-speeds have two derailleurs — a front system for the two front gears (called chainwheels) and a rear system for the five external rear gears (called the freewheel, the rear sprocket, or the rear cluster). There are ten possible separate combinations of the two front gears with the rear five. This gives the "ten-speed" its name.

The magical, sensual freedom of cycling flows from the derailleur and the ten gears. With the right combinations, the cyclist can go anywhere. On a hot day, riding alone up a long mountain road holds unexplainable joy. You maintain; you persist; you direct every muscle into pedaling, into forward, uphill motion. Sweat beads sting your eyes but you blink them out; your concentration peaks; you don't give up and nothing can stop you. The summit approaches, you can see how the road seems to end in midair as it drops off for its long downhill rush. You feel good, knowing that where man is now pulled by a fueled metal machine, you, with your power and determination, rode.

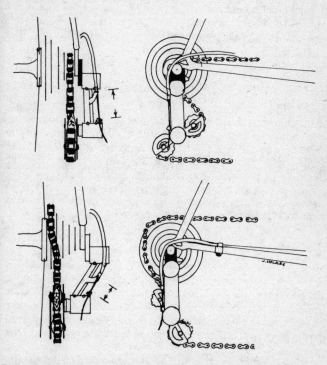

Fig. 2. During shifting, the derailleur moves in two planes to position the chain to the proper gear. Note the changes in the derailleur body and jockey-tension wheel cage when in a high gear (top) and a low gear (bottom).

Through the ten gears and derailleur, and with feet strapped tightly in the pedals and hands grasping the handlebars, you extend from your cycle and your cycle extends from you. Together you feel each bump in the road; together you sense the gradual change in the shape of the land; and together you take each sharp turn with perfect balance because you are balance —you and your cycle. Because you feel these things, you are no longer isolated or separated from nature. Instead, you are in the midst of it, and because of this, you can see the wholeness, the unity, the balance, and the mystery of it all. To attain this metaphysical thrill, get a Simplex, Campagnolo, or Huret derailleur.

Frame

The biggest difference between high- and low-quality bikes is in the frame. Poor-quality frames made from welded, heavy, unreinforced steel tubing are weak and easily strained. The best frames are made from a lightweight steel-chrome alloy called Reynolds 531. Braised at low temperatures to reduce brittleness, these tubes are reinforced through a method called butting—the tube ends are slightly thicker than the rest of the tube for added strength, and are "lugged" together, i.e., when joined, the tubes are fitted into special sleeves ("lugs") for

Fig. 3. Cross section of a Reynolds 531 double-butted tube. Note how the tube flares from a narrow center to wider, reinforced butted ends.

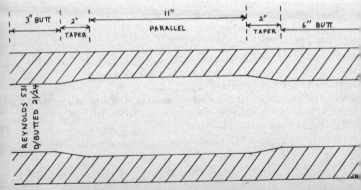

strength, flexibility, and responsiveness. (See figure 3.) When looking at frames, make sure to find one labeled, "Guaranteed built with Reynolds 531 butted *tubes, forks,* and *stays.*" There are three other frame types constructed with Reynolds 531 but they are not the best you can get, merely weaker hybrids.

On bicycles costing less than $200, little argument occurs over the question of quality between different brand-name parts. On bicycles costing $200 and more, the question of quality between different brand-name parts is a heated, esoteric debate. At the crux of the argument is the name Campagnolo. An Italian factory, Campagnolo, over the years developed the reputation of manufacturing the finest precision-made bicycle parts in the world. Today, parts made by Mafac, Normandy, Simplex, and Stronglight challenge and dispute that reputation, but despite the challenges and despite the lack of noticeable performance differences between Campagnolo and the other brand names, Campagnolo ("Campy" to those in the know) maintains its reputation and remains "the" parts to buy. Campagnolo accomplishes this either with its flawless steel, its simple and trouble-free design, its impeccable engineering and craftsmanship, or with its most obvious distinction — its outrageous prices.

Broadly speaking, there are three major bicycle types, each with its own price, particular use, and qualitative degree. Consequently, the prospective cyclist must be sure he chooses his cycle type correctly or he may find himself climbing a hill on a bike that feels as if it has square wheels and marshmallow bearings.

The cheapest, least precision made of the three bicycle types is the standard American prototype, the coaster-brake, balloon-tired tank. (See figure 4.) This obese bike, with its welded steel frame, is easy to ride and accepts constant abuse without complaint. Unmatched in sturdiness and raw strength, this machine is the Clydesdale of cycling, able to haul a seemingly unlimited amount of weight and able to travel over any type of terrain, be it sandy beach or a freshly fertilized suburban lawn. When decked out with clothespins, baseball cards, and colorful streamers and ridden full tilt downhill, its sound and sight are

Fig. 4. The Clydesdale of cycling: the balloon-tired, coaster-brake clunker.

enough to impress the Hell's Angels and the State Highway Patrol and tempt them both into chasing you for a closer look. The price range for this overweight, but fun-filled, American monstrosity runs from $10 to $60, and if your interest is a rugged bounce-about, this is the bike to get.

The lighter weight, more maneuverable English racer is the second bike type. (See figure 5.) Equipped with an internal three- or five-speed gear-changer, side-pull hand brakes, thin clincher tires, and a braised steel frame, this matronly cycle is best for riding about town between bridge club meetings and bingo games, or for short thirty- to forty-mile round-trip jaunts into the country to see your favorite adulterer. Do not be misled by the word *racer;* though better built than the American steel monster, it hasn't the quality or ability of the precision ten-speed. Constructed for moderate use over moderate terrain, the English racer is moderately priced, from $60 to $100. Look for models made by Schwinn, Dunelt, and Raleigh.

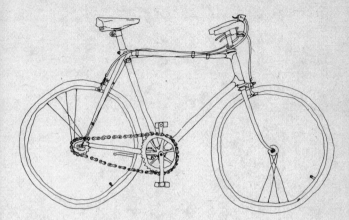

Fig. 5. The three-speed English Racer is not really a racer, but a cycle designed for gentle travel over moderate terrain.

The third cycle type is the ten-speed, which itself divides into three subcategories: the cheap, the moderately expensive, and the expensive.

The offspring of a bizarre ménage à trois involving the American tank, the English racer, and the European ten-speed, the "cheap" ten-speed is legitimate in name alone and is a bastard in its parts and quality. Costing from $49.99 to $79.99 and usually sold as holiday specials or given away at trailer park grand openings with balloons, doughnuts, and all the coffee you can guzzle, this bicycle is apt to fall apart and is breakage-prone. Pitifully weak and poorly constructed, the cheap ten-speed is good for riding back to wherever you bought it and asking for a refund.

Like the stretch of wet sand lying between the water's edge and the dry beach, the medium-quality, moderately expensive ten-speed is a meeting ground. Touched by only one finger from the hand of quality, this cycle is a combination of reliable parts, but nowhere approaches the precision machine. Usually cost-

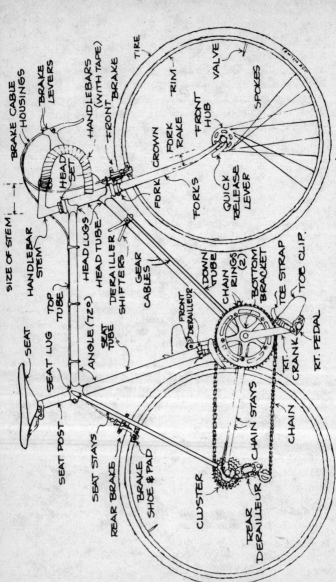

Fig. 6. The king of the road, the precision-built, outrageously expensive, quality ten-speed.

ing between $100 and $175, this bike has quick-release alloy hubs, alloy clincher rims, a braised steel-alloy frame (*not* Reynolds 531), cottered cranks, and a dependable derailleur system. In many cases these cycles are the little brothers to high-quality bikes (like the lower-quality Peugeot UO-8 to the Peugeot PX-10). Reliable, durable, sturdy, these bikes are good if your time and money are limited, if you need a strong machine for long-distance travel, or if you want a good bike for commuting to the office and, riding on weekends. For a good all-around bicycle, look for the Peugeot UO-8, the Gitane Gran Sport and Interclub, the Schwinn Sports Tourer and Super Sport, and the Raleigh Record, Grand Prix, and Super Course.

Looking like a contortionist's jungle gym, with its dropped, curved handlebars, and a masochist's wet dream, with its hard, narrow seat, the top quality ten-speed is a combination of strength, lightness, and flexibility. (See figure 6.) If the American balloon-tired tank is the workhorse of the bicycle world, the precision-crafted ten-speed is the thoroughbred. Costing $200 and above, these long-distance open-road racing machines give the rider the muscle to climb, the maneuverability to corner, and the speed to sprint. Having a lugged, double-butted Reynolds 531 frame, alloy center-pull brakes, aluminum cotterless cranks, quick-release alloy hubs, alloy rims, and sew-up tires, these machines are the essence of quality. And besides all that, they look good. Designed for racing, these cycles, when fitted for carrying special panniers and geared low, are a pleasure to tour on. The names to look for are Peugeot PX-10, Gitane Tour de France and Super Corsa, Cinelli, Masi, Mercier, Le Jeune, Louison-Bobet, and Schwinn Paramount.

Proper cycle frame size and correct gearing are determined by the last ingredient in bicycle selection: the buyer's physical size and condition.

A bicycle's frame size is measured from the seat post lug (the sleeve in which the vertical seat tube joins the horizontal top tube) to the center of the bottom bracket (where the axle emerges and connects to the crank). (See figure 7.) To determine your proper frame size, stand in stocking feet and measure your inseam. The frame for you is approximately nine or ten inches less than this measurement. With this rough estimate, visit a bicycle shop (a good point: visit a bicycle shop, not a department store or discount hardware shop), kick off your shoes, and ask to try on a bicycle. With your feet comfortably flat on the floor, as you straddle its top tube the bike should just touch in the crotch. If it doesn't and the gap difference is slight, little can be done; but do not despair, this slight difference has no effect on your cycling. If the gap between you and the top tube is extreme (more than two inches), you need a larger frame size. If the frame does more than touch (if it comes close to molesting you), you're in for serious trouble if you select this bike and make a fast, panic stop some rainy day on a slick road. Science has proved that no better way exists to keep the birth rate down than to provide healthy males with bicycles that are too large.

On a ten-speed, three types of gearing range are available. Called racing, touring, and alpine, these ranges are a particular arrangement of gear numbers often mistermed as "gear ratios," which designate the "highness" and "lowness" of a desired gear combination. Gear numbers are the result of dividing one of the five toothed gears on the rear cluster into one of the gears in front (in other words, into one of the chainwheels) and multiplying that number by the diameter of the bicycle's wheel (twenty-seven inches).

For example, with a rear cluster of 14, 16, 19, 24, and 28 teeth and two chainwheels of 38 and 52 teeth, the following gear range occurs:

(# of teeth)	(# of teeth) rear cluster	Gear range number
1st chainwheel = 38 ÷	14 = 2.71	= 73.2 (7th)
	16 = 2.37 x 27 (wheel diameter)	= 64.1 (6th)
	19 = 2	= 54 (4th)
	24 = 1.58	= 42.7 (2nd)
	28 = 1.35	= 36.6 (1st)
(# of teeth)		
2nd chainwheel = 52 ÷	14 = 3.71	= 100.3 (10th)
	16 = 3.25 x 27 (wheel diameter)	= 87.8 (9th)
	19 = 2.74	= 73.9 (8th)
	24 = 2.16	= 58.5 (5th)
	28 = 1.36	= 50.1 (3rd)

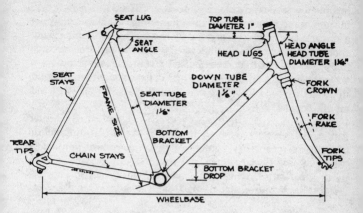

Fig. 7. The cycle's frame and its measurements. Frame size is measured from the seat post lug to the center of the bottom bracket.

The tube diameters shown are standard on most quality machines. Narrower or wider diameters should be avoided because they make frames too weak or too heavy.

Frame angles, particularly the head angle, affect maneuverability dramatically, with a steeper angle giving quicker handling. Three-speeds have a head angle of about 69 degrees, ten-speeds from 70 to 73 degrees, and track racing cycles 73 or 74 degrees.

Bottom bracket drop, measured from the wheel axle to the bracket's bottom, determines, with a given wheel size, how far you can lean and still pedal. Small drop is good for tight cornering, but big drop is more stable because of its low center of gravity.

Because unnecessary long tubing weakens a frame and adds weight, the shorter the cycle's wheelbase, the better. Forty-two inches is a common wheelbase length and is too long. Forty inches is better but is found only on expensive cycles.

Like frame angles, the fork rake affects handling. Without rake, riding no-handed would be impossible. With too much rake (as on a bike with a long wheelbase) the cycle will be unresponsive and unnecessarily soft on the bumps an American cyclist encounters.

Besides indicating the highness or lowness of a gear combination, gear numbers (or range numbers) are directly proportional to the distance traveled by the bicycle with one revolution of the cranks. In other words, to find out how far you'll travel in a particular gear, multiply the gear number by 3.14 (π). For example, in the chart, the distance traveled with one turn of the cranks when in third (or 50.1) is $50.1 \times 3.14 = 157.3$ or $157\frac{1}{4}$ inches.

Many people, including some cyclists, believe bicycle gearing is a linear progression similar to that of an automobile; that first gear on a cycle occurs when the chain is on the largest rear gear and the smaller chainwheel in the front; that shifting to the next largest rear gear gives second, shifting to the third largest gives third, and so on to fifth. Similarly, they believe gears six through ten result from shifting over to the larger front chainwheel and back to the largest rear cog and working up the rear sprocket again. As the chart indicates, this linear progression does not always hold true. In this instance, first and second are on the smaller chainwheel and the two largest rear gears, but third is not. To get third, the chain must be shifted over to the larger chainwheel and back to the largest rear gear. This is called a staggered gear progression. A good cycling tip is to figure out your gear range numbers, type them onto two small pieces of paper, and tape them close to the center of your handlebars for quick, easy reference.

Based on gear numbers, a racing gear range runs from the middle 50s to the low 100s. Very close, this range keeps the racing cyclist moving as fast as possible even when climbing grades. Riding in this gear range is strenuous and the beginner should avoid this range until his legs are strengthened. Touring gears start in the high 30s and run to 100. Designed for riding up and down long grades and over rapid terrain changes, this gearing is ideal for the unconditioned beginner as it makes learning to ride easy and builds endurance and strength. Alpine gearing, which begins in the low 30s, is designed for just what its name implies: climbing steep mountain roads.

After you've selected a bike on the basis of reputation and quality standards, and before you've taken it out of the shop, it is still worthwhile to check its parts to be certain a fluke hasn't slipped by. If you don't, you may find yourself the proud owner of a flashy, two-wheeled, ten-speed lemon.

Wheels

To check the wheels, have the cycle lifted to eye level. Spin the wheels and watch the rims (not the tires) as they whir between the brake shoe pads. A side wobble indicates that the wheel is "untrue" and that the spokes need to be tightened. Take a straight, narrow object and hold it horizontally just above the tire's edge. Again, spin the wheel, and watch it as it passes the hand-held object. If the wheel "jumps" or "hops," then it is "out-of-round" and the spokes need to be retightened.

Spokes

Pluck or twang the spokes of the wheel and listen to them. Their sounds should be closely similar and their feel should be equally taut.

Hubs

Spin the wheel slowly; it should stop gradually and evenly. Have someone hold the frame as you grasp the wheel and move it laterally. If it moves, there's "side play" and the hub cones need to be tightened.

Brakes

Spin the wheels and squeeze the brakes; they should brake evenly and should grab the rim squarely. Upon release, the pads should open cleanly and not rub the rim.

Gears

Turn the crank and shift the gears; the chain should shift quickly, evenly, and quietly. If there are loud, tinny noises or if the chain does not make it onto a gear, the derailleur needs readjustment.

Bottom Bracket and Cranks

Slip the chain off the small chainwheel onto the bottom bracket lug, and spin the cranks. They should spin freely, easily, and quietly and should stop gradually. If they don't, the bottom bracket cone is too tight. Next, grasp the cranks, one hand on each, and while someone holds the frame steady, try to move the crank from side to side; if it moves, the bottom bracket cone is too loose and needs tightening.

Frame

Stand in front of the cycle and sight down its frame. There should be no bends or twists. Closely inspect the paint around the lugs; wrinkled or buckled paint indicates the possibility of a damaged frame. Inspect the tubing as it enters the lugs; a bump or bunched fold reveals a damaged frame.

Once checked and purchased, the cycle needs to be fitted to the rider. If the salesman at the shop is too busy to aid you with this, you can do it yourself by following these simple methods:

Adjust your saddle so that you can sit on it and *fully* extend your right leg, *heel down,* to the pedal, as the pedal is in its lowest position. Because pedaling is done with the *ball* of the foot, your leg will be close to its full extension when you ride. Having your leg almost fully extended like this, utilizes the elasticity of the muscle and produces maximum muscle efficiency.

Another way to determine correct saddle height is to measure, as you stand shoeless, the distance from the crotch to the bottom of your foot. Multiply the measurement by 109 percent and you'll get the proper saddle height, scientifically. To set the saddle at this scientific height, measure from the top of the saddle down the seat tube to the pedal spindle as the crank is in its *fullest* extension, and adjust the seat post accordingly.

The proper distance between saddle and handlebars can be determined by placing your elbow at the saddle's nose and extending your forearm with hand and fingers outstretched to the handlebars. When your fingers just touch the back edge of the

Fig. 8. This lever-operated tricycle equipped with speed adjustments appeared in 1879—the first appearance of changeable speeds for cycles.

handlebars' center, you have the correct distance. Adjust the saddle to this distance by loosening the clip under it and moving the saddle horizontally. With a perfect fitting cycle, you'll be back in the saddle and ready to ride into the sunset.

The bicycle's first cousins are the unicycle and the tricycle, the former being exclusively reserved for neighborhood daredevils and circus showmen, the latter for years belonging to the domain of children. But recently the ubiquitous "trike" has become a favorite vehicle of post-retirement senior citizens.

Not to be outdone by young whippersnappers, the old folks have been creating a boom of their own.

Imagine, if you will, a panting pack of hefty, gray-haired matrons in blinding-bright orange ponchos, on rainbow-splashed tricycles, weaving down a palm-treed boulevard under a pastel-blue Florida sky. Above the matrons' ancient heads, on wiggling antennae that shoot from the trikes, floats the tricycling tribe's trademark: small luminous orange balls. Who are these three-wheeling old ladies? Grandmothers of the Hell's Angels trying to bridge the generation gap? Paid promoters of the orange grower's industry? Nuts? No, just the Moonbeams, an informal Floridian community organization of elderly folk put to pasture who find traveling on three wheels an enjoyable, safe, and healthy way to move. The Moonbeams and their enthusiasm are examples of the "trike trend" sweeping planned communities of trailer parks and mobile homes in Southern California, Arizona, and Florida.

Planted in the soil of early retirement, the adult trike boom draws nourishment from the emphasis on physical fitness, the increasing number of planned communities for the retired, and the simple fact that tricycles are easy and cheap to operate and maintain. The trend blossoms in the planned communities where the development's little-traveled but well-paved level roads inspire relaxing rides at sunset or invigorating morning jaunts to the grocery store. And, as one mobile home park manager and trike enthusiast points out, the grown-up three-wheeler "stimulates community identity and encourages retirees to build new lives and friendships instead of sitting around home moping about times past and complaining about times present."

Adult tricycles are ideal for grown-ups who never learned how to ride and want to, or who are limited by physical handicap or old age. The trikes come in three gear ranges: a fixed gear, which means the pedals revolve with every revolution of the rear wheel, making pedaling easier for individuals with weak legs because the wheel's revolution pulls the pedal around—(also, because the fixed gear permits back-pedaling, the rider can back up as well as ride forward, a technique that is a lifesaver in tight spots), and two- and three-speed models that enable low-gear cycling over terrain of moderate incline. All models come with a large, removable rear basket, a front caliper hand brake, and 27″ or 26″ x 1¾″ wheels. A kit for converting a bicycle into an adult trike is available from Workman's Cycles of Brooklyn and costs between $70 and $90, depending on wheel size. The price range for a complete grown-up tricycle ranges from about $120 for the single-speed, fixed-gear model to $150 for the three-speed. Tricycle manufacturers enjoying the business boom are the Schwinn Bicycle Company, Workman's Cycles, and Alco Cycle Products in Florida.

Accessories

Bicycle accessories, besides functional value, have class, and they're fun to buy and involve you with your machine. Some accessories are essential and should be purchased with the cycle; others are refinements, and can be bought as the beginning cyclist recognizes his cycling abilities, and as he realizes the type of cycling he prefers.

Air Pump. A good air pump, made by Zefal or Campagnolo (the Impero model), is a necessity for sew-up tires. Costing between $5 and $7, these pumps give one hundred pounds of air pressure. Pumping a sew-up is simple, except the valves are extremely delicate and snap easily. Caution should be exercised. When in the 12:00 o'clock position, open the valve by unscrewing its stem counterclockwise. Carefully press and fit the pump head over the valve and, with the wheel held steady to avoid snapping the valve stem, start pumping at a regular, smooth pace, without erratic side play. When the desired pressure is reached, knock the pump straight off the valve with a quick, downward blow from the side of your fist and close the valve. Because clincher tires require less air pressure and use a standard valve, they can be filled easily with any conventional $5 bicycle pump.

Shraeder Adapter. Sew-up tires come with a European Presta valve that doesn't fit standard American gasoline station air hoses; because of this, the little 25¢ Shraeder tire valve adapter is a lifesaver. When using a gas station hose, open the Presta valve and screw on the Shraeder adapter. Carefully inflate the sew-up with short bursts of air, and after each burst, squeeze the tire to measure hardness. If the air hose has a gauge, use it but don't rely on it. Gas station gauges are reliably inaccurate. When finished, remove the adapter, close the Presta valve, and screw the adapter back on. It will ride safely on the wheel.

Hand Tire Gauges. Dependable and accurate, the hand gauge can be bought in any automotive shop or hardware store. Sew-up tire owners should find the type gauge that registers air pressure to 125 pounds, and fits the Shraeder adapter. Clincher tire owners need only buy conventional automobile tire gauges, which cost about $1.25.

Nail Puller. A must for sew-up tires. Lightweight and out of the way, this small tire accessory bolts over the rear tire and scrapes off bits of glass, thorns, sharp rocks, nails, and other nasties that want to pop tires.

Tire Repair Kit. It is the cyclist's destiny to have a flat tire. When it comes, be ready with a tire patch kit. For sew-up tires, find kits made by Velox or Clement. Check the kits for thread, needle, patches, glue, sandpaper, and thimble. The cost is about $1.25. For clincher tires, pick up any standard tire repair kit found in bike shops coast to coast.

Toe Clips. For better cycling efficiency, toe clips are the accessory to have. They keep the ball of the foot positioned on the pedal and allow the cyclist to pull the pedals up and take full advantage of the leg muscles. When riding in traffic, keep the clips open for quick foot removal, and for even greater cycling efficiency, use the clips with shoe cleats, an accessory that keeps the foot from slipping out of the pedal and allows the cyclist to apply more pressure directly on the pedal.

Cycling Shoes, Jersey, Shorts, Gloves, and Helmet. All these items, which can be purchased in most top-quality bike shops, facilitate cycling. Lightweight, flexible cycling shoes keep the foot comfortable while pedaling, and when used with cleats, they increase cycling efficiency. There are two shoe types: a lightweight racing type that will not stand heavy abuse, and a more durable, but still lightweight, style used for general cycling. Both cost up to $20.

The cycling jersey is a short-sleeved, heavy, stretchable knit shirt with large back pockets that hold anything from a bagged lunch to a spare tire. The shorts are tight and stretchable, permitting full leg movement without binding or chafing. Cycling gloves are of wide knit, for protection from blisters and scrapes, and cover half the hand, allowing complete finger freedom. The helmet is of leather straps for lightness, strength, and bounce-ability.

To the serious cyclist, these clothing items are essential; for the casual rider, they are dispensable. Using them makes cycling easier, safer, and more dashing.

Water Bottles. For long-distance touring and racing, a water bottle is a must. (See figure 9.) Costing about $4.50 with its mounting cage, the bottle can be placed within the rider's easy reach without interference to his cycling. It comes with two head caps — one, a drinking spout, and the other, a shower spray. On long-distance tours, particularly in the summer, carry two bottles.

Cloth Handlebar Tape. On many new cycles, the handlebars are covered with a vinyl, plasticlike tape that to some cyclists is uncomfortable. Costing about 75¢ a roll (two rolls are needed to tape the handlebars) and available in most cycle shops, textured cloth tape is easier to grip, and comes in a kaleidoscope of colors. When on the cycle, the tape acts like a racing stripe on a car: it makes it go faster.

Rear Carrying Rack. For hauling books to classes, groceries from the store, or panniers filled with your worldly possessions, a die-cast steel carrier made by the Swiss factory, Pletscher, is best. It costs about $6 and attaches easily to the cycle's seat stays and rear fork ends. To save your cycle's paint job and to minimize slippage, place strips of old inner tube under the carrier's securing brackets, as you attach the rack to the stays.

Leg Lamp. A popular accessory, this small lamp straps to the cyclist's leg or arm and does not interfere with cycling, as opposed to generator lamps that work off tire friction and make pedaling harder. A leg lamp performs two safety functions at once: it throws a light ahead and a red warning glow behind. It costs about $2.75, batteries included. (See figure 10.) Leg lamps are the key to safe night riding because there isn't a motorist living crazy enough to run over something that has one red eye and hops up and down in the middle of the night.

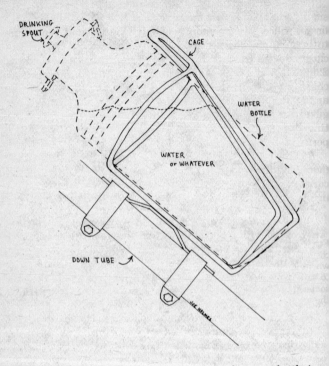

Fig. 9. For long-distance touring or for racing, the water bottle is a must. With mounting cage, the bottle costs about $4.50.

Chain and Lock. Sadly, for these days, a lock has to be considered the most important accessory. The Mill Valley (California) police, in a community of only ten thousand, report up to three hundred cycles stolen in a year. "And it's mainly because of ineffectual locks," said the officer. "People go and buy a $200 bike and a $2 lock to protect it." A case-hardened steel chain, long enough to go around the bike frame, rear wheel, and a fixed object, with a top-quality padlock, is the safest. To guarantee full cycle protection, keep your cycle in sight at all times, no matter where you are. If you are forced to leave it, periodically check on it, if possible.

Bicycle Carriers. The "now" thing is to have your cycle mounted like some taxidermic trophy on your car. Several carriers are available to afford you this thrill and they range in cost, size, and function (some fold up). The general cost range

Fig. 10. The leg lamp is lightweight, dependable, uses two batteries, costs about $2.75, and throws a white light ahead of you and a red warning glow behind. It is worn on the cyclist's left side and is the key to safe night riding because no motorist is crazy enough to run over something that has one red eye and hops up and down in the middle of the night.

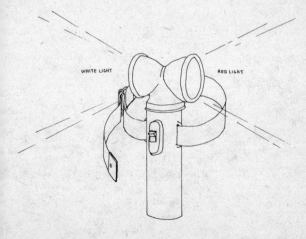

WHITE LIGHT   RED LIGHT

for the average aluminum bumper-secured cycle carrier is from $12 to $23. A rooftop carrier can be had for $30, or you can build one yourself cheaply from scrap wood, and attach it to the car's roof with aluminum alloy gutter brackets made by Quik-n-Easy Products of Monrovia, California.

4 *Riding a Bicycle*

> *"Some people ride bicycles effortlessly, while others must summon up the strength to ride. Some people have no fear while riding, while others tremble with each pedal-push. The true bicycle rider is neither strong nor weak, neither heroic nor cowardly, for he is one with his machine and thus beyond the pale of mundane considerations."*
>
> — Anonymous Wheelman, circa 1872

Ah, the brand-new cycle. How it glitters! How it gleams! How it impresses the little girl down the street. . . . How do I ride it?

Have no fear, riding a ten-speed is easy, all that's required is practice, care, and concentration. But before you learn how to jump on your cycle and pedal over the horizon, you must become a safety addict and develop the habit of safety checking pranksterlike parts each time you intend to cycle. A simple way of doing this is by asking yourself these questions:

Do the tires have air? Be a tire squeezer. Cotton sew-ups with conventional rubber tubing "breathe" and need daily doses of air. Squeeze the tire and check for its hardness. If soft, inflate to its proper pressure: for sew-ups, between eighty-five and one hundred pounds, and for clinchers, about seventy pounds.

Is the rear wheel true? Because of the constant pull and strain from chain and cranks, the rear-wheel quick-release hub can work itself free. When it does, the rear wheel jams into the left section of the stay and makes riding dangerous, if not impossible. To avoid this, keep the rear wheel straight in its stay, and keep the quick-release hub tight in the fork ends.

Do the brakes work? Leaving the cycle anywhere for any length of time makes it prey for prying fingers. Test your brakes before riding. Do they open cleanly? Without brakes, the cyclist is like a meteor spinning wildly through space, destined to plummet to the earth.

Are you in the gear you want? Riding from a high-number

gear combination is like running in cement tennis shoes. For easy, fast starts, use a low-gear combination. Get in the practice of gearing down each time you intend to stop and leave your cycle.

Now you're ready to learn the techniques of riding: (1) mounting, (2) shifting, (3) ankling, and (4) cadence.

When first attempted, mounting a cycle with toe-clipped pedals seems as hard as teaching a brown bear to ride a unicycle: it's clumsy and almost impossible. But stay with it, because, with practice, mounting can be done easily and smoothly. To mount, open the toe-clipped pedals *wide*, straddle the top tube, and insert your left foot in the pedal when it is in the 10:00 o'clock position. Then, in one quick motion, push off with your right foot, push down on the pedal with your left, pull yourself up with the handlebars, and sit on the saddle as you coast. Once on the saddle, insert your right foot in the empty pedal when it is in the 12:00 o'clock position. Pedal several times to keep your momentum, and as each pedal comes to its 12:00 o'clock position, reach down and pull the toe-clip strap tight. Mastering this technique takes time, but is worth it, because when done correctly, you'll look and ride like a pro.

To learn how to shift, lift the cycle off the ground or turn it upside down, balancing it on its seat and handlebars. Turn the cranks and run through the gears (an important point: the cranks must *always* be moving when shifting gears!), shifting both derailleurs. Select different gears and shift to those gears, or better yet, have a friend call out a gear (first, second, third, and so on) and shift to the called gear.

Note how the derailleur system works: when pulled down, or toward you as you sit on the cycle, the lever on the right side of the cycle (the side with the gears) shifts the *rear* derailleur and chain horizontally to the *left* (or to lower gears). When pushed up, or away from you, the lever shifts the derailleur to the right (or to higher gears).

The lever on the cycle's left side shifts the front derailleur. Pulling down on the lever moves the chain to the *right* (or onto the larger outside chainwheel) and pushing up, or away, on it shifts the derailleur and chain to the left, or to the lower gear, inside chainwheel. As you shift remember this: right lever is rear, left lever is front. Down on right gives "low," down on left gives "high."

Once familiar with the gearing, select a low-gear number, mount the cycle and ride a short distance over an area free of traffic. As you ride, sense your relationship with your cycle, particularly in balance and sitting posture.

Brake every twenty-five yards; it should be done smoothly and easily without shuddering or skidding. After ten or fifteen minutes of this introductory riding, remove your right hand from the handlebars and touch the right gear lever. Do this several times, alternating hands and gear levers.

After doing this and feeling secure, reach down to the gear lever and relieve pedaling pressure; don't stop pedaling, just ease up on the pedals. When your hand and leg movements are coordinated, reach down to the lever, ease pedaling pressure and shift gears. That's all there is to it; with practice, you'll be ready for the Rockies.

The most important riding technique is ankling, a method of maximizing leg muscle use by keeping the ball of the foot on the pedal during the entire stroke. (See figure 11.) The ankle's

Fig. 11. Ankling, a method of maximizing leg muscle use by keeping the ball of the foot on the pedal during the entire stroke, is the most important riding technique. Ankling with toe clips that allow the rider to pull up as well as push down on the pedals increases pedaling efficiency 30 to 50 percent.

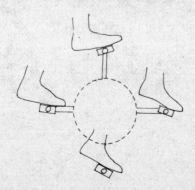

DISTANCE TRAVELED CHART

$$\frac{\text{chainwheel teeth}}{\text{freewheel teeth}} \times 27'' \times 3.14 = \text{distance traveled per revolution}$$

chain wheel / free-wheel	24	26	28	30	32	34	36	38	40	42	44	45	46	47	48	49	50	52	53	54	55	56
28	72.5	78.5	84.8	90.7	96.7	103.0	109.3	114.9	121.2	127.2	133.1	136.3	139.4	142.2	145.4	148.2	151.7	157.3	160.5	163.3	166.4	169.6
26	78.2	84.8	91.1	98.0	104.2	110.8	117.4	124.0	130.3	136.9	143.5	146.6	150.1	153.2	156.7	159.8	163.3	169.7	172.7	175.8	179.3	182.4
25	81.3	87.9	94.8	101.7	108.6	115.2	122.1	128.7	135.6	142.6	149.1	152.6	156.1	159.5	162.7	166.1	169.9	176.5	179.6	183.1	186.5	189.7
24	84.8	91.7	98.9	105.8	113.0	119.9	127.2	134.4	141.3	148.5	155.4	159.2	162.7	166.1	169.6	173.0	176.8	183.7	187.1	190.6	194.1	197.8
23	88.2	95.8	103.0	110.5	117.8	125.3	133.1	140.0	147.6	154.8	162.0	165.8	169.6	173.3	176.8	180.6	184.6	191.5	195.3	199.7	202.5	206.3
22	92.3	100.2	107.7	115.5	123.1	130.6	138.8	146.3	154.2	161.7	169.6	173.3	177.4	180.9	184.9	188.7	193.1	200.3	204.1	207.9	212.0	215.7
21	96.7	104.9	113.0	121.2	129.1	137.2	145.7	153.5	161.4	169.6	177.7	181.8	185.6	189.7	193.7	197.8	202.2	210.1	213.9	217.9	222.1	226.1
20	101.7	110.2	118.7	127.2	135.6	144.1	152.9	161.1	169.6	178.0	186.5	190.9	195.0	199.1	203.5	207.9	212.3	220.4	224.5	228.9	233.9	237.4

chain wheel / free wheel	24	26	28	30	32	34	36	38	40	42	44	45	46	47	48	49	50	52	53	54	55	56
19	107.1	115.5	124.7	133.8	142.9	151.3	160.5	169.6	178.4	187.5	196.2	201.0	205.4	216.0	214.1	218.5	223.6	232.0	236.4	240.8	245.2	249.6
18	113.0	122.5	131.9	141.3	150.7	160.1	169.6	179.0	188.4	197.8	207.2	212.0	216.7	221.4	226.1	230.8	235.8	244.9	249.6	254.3	259.0	263.8
17	119.6	129.4	139.4	149.5	159.5	169.6	179.6	189.3	199.4	209.4	219.5	224.5	229.5	234.2	239.3	244.3	249.6	259.4	264.1	269.1	274.1	279.1
16	127.2	137.8	148.2	158.9	169.6	179.6	191.2	201.3	212.0	222.6	233.3	238.6	243.7	249.0	254.3	259.7	265.3	275.7	280.7	286.1	291.4	296.7
15	135.6	147.0	153.2	169.6	180.9	191.8	203.5	214.8	226.1	237.4	248.7	254.0	260.0	265.6	271.3	276.9	282.9	293.9	299.6	305.2	310.9	316.5
14	145.1	157.3	169.6	181.5	193.7	205.7	218.2	230.2	242.1	254.3	266.6	272.2	278.5	284.5	290.8	296.7	303.3	314.9	320.9	326.9	332.8	339.1
13	156.4	169.6	182.4	195.6	208.5	221.7	234.6	247.7	260.9	273.8	287.0	293.3	299.9	306.5	313.1	319.7	326.6	339.1	345.4	352.0	358.6	365.2
12	169.9	183.7	197.8	212.0	226.1	240.2	254.7	268.5	282.6	296.7	310.9	317.8	325.0	331.9	339.1	346.0	353.9	367.4	374.6	381.5	388.4	395.6

Fig. 12. To find mph, multiply distance traveled by rpms, divide by 12 inches, multiply that answer by 60 minutes, and divide that answer by 5,280 feet.

rubber-bandlike tendons, combined with leg strength, pull the pedal up as the opposing foot pushes down. Ankling with toe clips, which keep the foot properly placed and tightly strapped to the pedal, increases pedaling efficiency approximately 30 percent.

To ankle, return to the area free of traffic and observe your ankle and foot as you ride: at the top of your pedal stroke, your heel should be slightly lower than your toes (this position gives efficient downward push). In the 3:00 o'clock position, your toes should angle slightly *lower* than your heel; at the bottom of your stroke, your foot should be in a forty-five-degree angle, with your heel *higher* than your toes; and you should hold this angle until the 10:00 o'clock pedal position.

Maintaining a relatively constant number of crank revolutions per minute is the key to enjoyable and efficient cycling. Called cadence, this technique of pedaling at a steady rate is achieved through proper use of the ten gears. To determine your natural cadence, find a gear that is comfortable to ride in, that is, a gear in which you can turn the cranks without strain, yet still meet with *slight* resistance.

As you pedal in this gear, count how many times you turn the cranks in a minute, while pacing yourself for the maximum time before tiring. The figure you come up with is your natural cadence, and when you are forced to shift because of grade steepness, road condition, your physical condition, wind velocity, or load weight, you should shift to *maintain* that cadence. Doing so will save you from the wear and tear that many cyclists go through by pedaling fast one minute and slow the next.

The cadence rate aids you in another manner: by multiplying the revolutions per minute times the distance traveled in a particular gear, you'll find out how fast you're going, and that is always a neat thing to know.

To save hours of mathematics, use the Distance Traveled Chart. (See figure 12.) The figures across the top of the chart indicate the number of teeth on the chainwheel. The figures down the left side indicate the number of teeth on the rear cog; the distance in inches traveled when in a particular gear are shown underneath the chainwheel and rear gear sizes. To find miles per hour, multiply the distance traveled by the number of revolutions per minute (cadence rate), divide the answer by 12 inches, multiply that answer by 60 minutes, and divide by 5,280 feet. For example, if you're riding on a rear cog of 17 teeth and a front chainwheel of 24, you travel 119.6 inches with each turn of the crank. With a cadence of 60 rpms, you travel 7,176 inches a minute, or, 598 feet a minute, which equals 34,880 feet an hour. Your speed is 5,280 divided into 34,880, or about 6.6 mph. You're whizzing right along.

5 Mechanics and Repairs

A new bicycle is indeed a thing of beauty. It twinkles, sparkles, and delights. It affords its rider the opportunity to pursue an entirely unique notion of grace. For months on end, one moves and marvels at the motion. Speed and silence combined, a rare synthesis. So rare and perfect, in fact, that the first stuttering loose bolt or squealing chain sounds, to an enthusiast, like a lover's painful confession. The end of an affair.

What to do but pick up the pieces? Though great owner/bicycle relationships are truly emotional undertakings, the situation differs from a standard contretemps in that one of the participants is a machine, hence facilitating reconciliation. It is easier to mend a derailleur than a broken heart, especially with a handy, step-by-step guide such as the one that begins on the very next page.

The sections in this chapter are arranged alphabetically and include:

All the repairs and overhauls in this chapter can easily be accomplished with the following tools:

6" Adjustable Wrench	6" Vice Grips
Large 12" Adjustable Wrench or Channel-lock Pliers	Chain Rivet Remover
	Small Screwdriver
Hammer (preferably hard rubber or wood)	Freewheel Remover
	Awl or Punch
Cotterless Crank Remover	Cone Wrenches
5 mm Allen Wrench	Spoke Wrench
Mafac Brake Tools	Tire Irons for Clinchers
Pliers with Wire Cutters	Tire Repair Kit

You may or may not need all these tools, or you may want more specialized equipment. Remember that tools enable you to communicate with your bike on a long-term basis and are always a good investment.

It's important to make an early distinction between the types of lubricant used on the various parts of the bike, and to mention some reputable brand names. When lightweight household oil is mentioned, this means an oil similar to 3-in-1 oil, such as Sturmey-Archer bicycle oil or Texaco Household Oil. Light oil or No. 10 machine oil refers to a heavier oil, such as Singer Sewing Machine Oil (but not as heavy as automobile crankcase oil). When grease is called for, any high-speed silicon grease will do. The best greases are Lubriplate No. 110 and Campagnolo, which tend to stay in the bearing races longer than Schwinn bicycle grease.

This chapter will be primarily concerned with the maintenance and repair of ten-speed bicycles, but the information can be put to specific use by the owners of five-speeds, three-speeds, and the American tank. The concepts are alike, only the details differ.

Working on a bicycle is always much easier when it is at eye level and when the wheels can be spun. If there are trees, overhangs, or rafters, the bike can be suspended by the handlebars and the saddle. If not, a simple rack can be built with scrap wood. (See figure 13.)

There are a great number of specialized tools that make bicycle repair easy. (Some are shown in figure 14.) None of these,

Fig. 13. A simple rack built from scrap wood. The clamp is secured with old inner tubes. A V-groove is cut in both pieces, 18 inches from the post and situated about 54 inches from the ground. It can also be extended from a workbench.

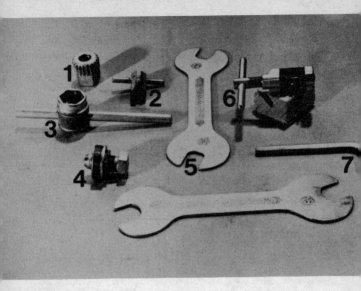

Fig. 14. Some good tools to have for maintenance of a top quality bike: (1) freewheel remover, (2) spoke wrench, (3) hexed cotterless crank bolt installer, (4) cotterless crank extractor and hexed extractor bolt, (5) cone wrenches, (6) chain rivet remover, and (7) 5 mm Allen wrench.

except the cotterless crank remover, are so essential that they couldn't be replaced with a simpler tool. The problem is that with continued use, the simpler tools tend to chew up the bicycle. There are a great deal of grease-cutting solvents on the market, but kerosene is good for grease, oil, and gunk, while white gas is good for rubber, glue, and tar. But like most solvents, these aren't good for skin or viscera.

Bottom Bracket and Cranks

The bottom bracket (see figure 15) consists of axle, bearings, and cones. This cone-bearing relationship is found throughout the bicycle: bottom bracket, headset, hubs, pedals, and derailleur wheels. If the axle is wobbly or difficult to turn, there is a good chance that the cones are out of adjustment. The bottom bracket has a fixed cone on the chainwheel side and an adjustable cone, with a lock ring, on the opposite side. By screwing the adjustable cone in or out, it is possible to minimize side play, or wobble, and to maximize free rotation. Tightening the lock ring often changes the adjustment; so trial and error will be the best method in becoming an experienced cone-bearing man.

Cottered cranks (see figure 16) often work themselves loose. If you have a loose crank, support the axle on a block of wood and hammer the cotter bolt in with another piece of wood. Then tighten the nut on the other end of the cotter.

Lubrication. Generally speaking, the bottom bracket should

Fig. 15. An exploded view of the bottom bracket, consisting of: (1) cranks, (2) chainwheels, (3) dust caps, (4) axle bolts, (5) bottom brackets bearing, (6) axle, (7) removable bearing cone (the other cone is permanently set in the frame), and (8) lock ring. Note: the machine-tooled end sections of the axle are of different lengths, designed to compensate on the right side for the extra width added by the chainwheels.

Fig. 16. A cottered crank (1) is secured to the axle (2) by a wedgelike cotter bolt (3). Also shown is the front derailleur cage (4) correctly following the curve of the chainwheel, and the outward-limit adjusting screw (5).

be regreased once a year. In order to get at the bottom bracket, you have to go through the cranks—either cottered or cotterless. From the repairman's point of view, the only difference between the two is the method of removal and replacement.

Cottered Cranks. To disassemble cottered cranks, remove the nut from the cotter bolt in the crank opposite the chainwheel. (See figures 16 and 17.) Note the direction that the cotter goes through the crank, support the axle, and pound the bolt out with a piece of wood. If it doesn't budge, put the nut onto the top threads and try again. (If forced to use a hammer,

Fig. 17. Cross section of a cottered crank revealing how the cotter bolt or ("pin") holds the crank on the axle. Removing the bolt without damage is tricky.

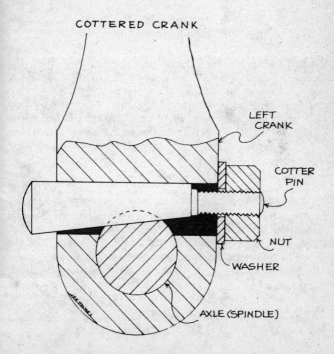

you may have to replace the cotter bolt.) Remove the crank and the lock ring with channel lock pliers, screwdriver, and hammer, or a Raleigh spanner. By holding a cup under the bracket, you may not lose too many of the bearings as the adjustable cone is being removed. It is best to do this when the bike is upright—the bearings love to slide into the tubes that are connected to the bottom bracket. Next, unscrew the fixed cone and extract the axle, chainwheel, crank, and the other half of the bearings. Count the bearings and soak them in kerosene.

Cotterless Cranks. (See figure 18.) To disassemble cotterless cranks, unscrew the dust caps on each crank arm—if the cap is slotted, use a screwdriver; if it's keyholed, use a 5 mm Allen hex key. Remove the exposed axle bolts with the socket of the installer tools. Thread the extractor into the dust-cap threads and screw down the extractor post with the socketed installer. (See figure 14.) When the crank is loose, pull it straight off the axle. Take off both cranks. The rest is the same as the cottered crank except that there is no need to remove the fixed cone.

After the bottom bracket has been disassembled, clean all the parts with kerosene. The more surgically this is done, the more ecstatic you'll be when riding up those long hills. (Many people like to seal the frame tube openings by installing a tin can liner.) Regrease the cones and axles with high-speed bicycle grease or Lubriplate No. 110. Be liberal with the grease.

Reassembly is simply the reverse of disassembly except that you are working against gravity instead of with it. On the cottered cranks, line the fixed cone with grease, coat the axle, and set the bearings in the cone. Push the axle and bearings against the cone and screw the cone into the bracket. Then do the same for the adjustable cone—the grease should hold the bearings in place while you move it over the axle. On the cotterless cranks it's the same except that the bearings on the fixed cone are stuck to the axle with grease and then the axle is carefully pushed through the bottom bracket.

Adjust the cones so there is minimal side play and maximum free spinning. Tighten the lock ring and check the cone adjustment. If everything is all right, replace the crank(s). New cotter bolts should have a bevel, but the bevel may have to be increased before it will fit. (See figure 19.)

Fig. 18. Cotterless cranks are held to the axle by bolts, one of which remains hidden by the keyholed dust cap and can only be removed with a crank extractor tool. (See figure 14.)

Fig. 19. A new cotter bolt may be too wide to fit in the axle mechanism. To make it fit, increase its bevel by filing the bolt down from the blunt end to the threads.

Troubleshooting:

Wobbly Axle or Cranks. First check for loose cranks. If these are tight, look for a loose lock ring (see figure 15), which would indicate loose cones. If the lock ring is tight, try readjusting the cones. Still no luck? Overhaul the bottom bracket and check for missing bearings or a bent axle. The next stop is the bike shop.

Squeaking Noise. Check for loose cranks or loose cones. Next, try cleaning and oiling the pedals. If that doesn't work, the bottom bracket needs overhauling.

Grinding Noises. Clean chainwheel and chain, looking for chain wear or burrs on the teeth of the chainwheel. If this isn't the problem, clean and lubricate the pedals. Beyond this, the solution lies in a bottom bracket overhaul. Check the bearings and cones for pitting and grooves.

Cranks Are Hard to Turn. Loosen the cones or overhaul the bottom bracket.

Brakes

Side-pull and center-pull brakes are adjusted either through an adjustment screw located on the body of the brake, along the cable, or by pulling the brake cable through the anchor bolt. (See figures 20, 21, and 23.) The brakes should be adjusted so that the pads are as close to the rim as possible without dragging, and such that the surface of the brake pad squarely hits the surface of the rim. Brake pads should be replaced when

Fig. 20. This side-pull brake shows (1) adjusting nut attached to the center bolt, (2) adjustment screw, and (3) anchor bolt. Note that the open ends of the brake shoe face toward the rear of the bike.

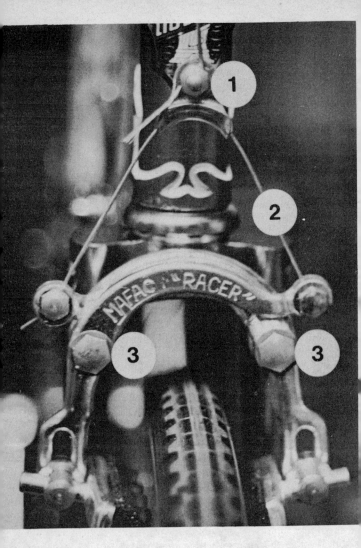

Fig. 21. A center-pull brake showing (1) anchor bolt, (2) yoke, and (3) pivot bolts. The closed ends of the brake shoes face forward.

they get worn or hard. (See figure 35.) To remove the brake pad, it is often easier to twist it out with a pair of pliers than to try to slide it out. New pads, however, are given to sliding, and the metal stop should be pointed forward in order to hold the brake pad during stops.

Brake levers should be placed where they offer the greatest number of comfortable hand positions. People with small hands may find it difficult to use normally adjusted brakes, so here is a suggestion for shortening the gap. The trick is to eliminate part of the post on the lever side. With a round file or a drill equipped with a small Carborundum stone, grind up to one-half inch off the brake post, following the curve of the original. (See figure 22.) Then with a small flat file, remove the

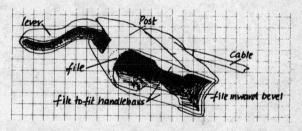

Fig. 22. Bottom view of brake lever.

metal inside, which interferes with a close fit, and put an inward bevel on the opposite curve. It may be necessary to shorten the lever securing bolt (see figure 23), which is inside the post, but that is easily done with a hacksaw and then smoothing the cut with a flat file.

Lubrication. The moving parts of the brakes and levers should be lubricated occasionally with lightweight household oil. If you keep your cables oiled, they won't rust. Frayed cables should be replaced, and oil should be kept away from pads and rims—for safety's sake.

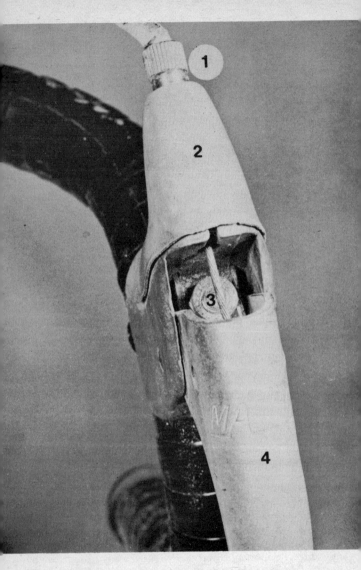

Fig. 23. A Mafac brake lever showing (1) cable adjustment screw, (2) brake post, (3) brake lever securing bolt, and (4) lever.

Troubleshooting:

Squishy Brakes. Move the brake pads closer to the rim, with the adjusting screw or cable, and check for worn pads. Make sure the cable is not slipping through the anchor bolt. (See figures 20 and 21.)

Squealing Brakes. Old, hardened brake pads often squeal. If your pads are in good shape, take a look at the rims for any rubber or glue, which may cause the squealing—the rims can be cleaned with white gas. Next to living with the noise, the last solution is to toe-in the brake pads by either slightly bending the front part of the arms toward the rim or by trimming the back part of the pad with a razor blade.

Shuddering Brakes. Check for a loose center bolt (see figure 20) on the brake or for dinged rims. Sometimes glue or rubber on the rims can cause shuddering. If it's none of these, check for a loose front hub or headset. (See *Hubs* or *Headset.*)

Sticky Brakes. If the brakes apply or release in a jerky fashion, check the ends of the spaghetti loops for burrs, which may catch the cable. It could be catching at or inside the brake lever, or the brake lever could be catching on the post, in which case oil and gently pry it free.

For side-pull brakes, try working some oil into the center bolt and make sure the brake arms are not binding on one another. If the brake still sticks, try loosening the adjusting nut (see figure 20), and make sure that the locknut is set against the adjusting nut rather than the brake arm. Beyond that, check for a bent center bolt. For sticky center-pull brakes, oil the pivots and check for bent brake arms. Other than that, you may have bent pivot bolts (see figure 21), which may or may not be repairable—take it to a bike shop.

Brake Doesn't Release. Check for binding cables and levers (see *Sticky Brakes*). If only one pad refuses to release on a side-pull brake, there is a good chance that the center bolt is too loose, is too tight and in the wrong position. A dragging brake pad may also be due to a weak spring on the side that drags. (See figure 20.) Take a screwdriver and gently bend the spring upward, on the dragging side. If this doesn't work, get center-pull brakes. If one shoe on a center-pull brake doesn't release, it's probably because the center bolt and bridge are in the wrong position—straighten your brake.

Slow Stops. Check for worn pads or greasy pads and rims. You may want to change from smooth to knurled rims.

Chain

Ideally, the chain should move easily and solidly through the gears, should be free of vibration and noise, and should not sag. A short chain will be difficult to get onto the large chainwheel and the large cog of the freewheel. A long chain will have very little tension when it's on the small chainwheel and the small cog of the freewheel. If your chain is loose, but not loose enough to remove a link, try moving the wheel farther back into the stays. You may have a worn chain that needs replacing.

Lubrication. The chain should be kept free of abrasive dirt, and it is best cleaned and oiled when removed from the bicycle. Removal can be achieved with a chain rivet remover (see figure 14) or with a hammer and punch. Clean the chain with kerosene and an old toothbrush or paintbrush, and wipe dry. The chain can then be lubricated with one of four materials: No. 10 machine oil, paraffin, silicon spray, or graphite. If you use oil or paraffin, soak the chain and remove the excess.

Troubleshooting (also see *Bottom Bracket and Cranks, Chainwheel, Derailleur—Front and Rear,* and *Pedals*):

Worn Chain. Your chain should be replaced when the riveted joints become worn, which is also known as "stretch." The best indication of this is the horizontal deflection, or bending, of the chain perpendicular to its motion. If the top portion of the chain can be pushed horizontally into the spokes, when on the large chainwheel and the middle cog of the freewheel, you may have a worn chain. Remove the chain, lay it with the rivets horizontal, and gently bend it into a tight, smooth curve (keeping the rivets parallel to the surface). If the cord length— distance from each end—is less than two-thirds the linear length, you need a new chain. To make sure, take a short segment of the chain and lay it out straight. By pushing and pulling, without flexing it, a worn chain will show considerable play where a good chain will barely show any.

Replacing Chain. If you decide to install a new chain, take the old one and stretch it out on a two-by-four, nailing both ends down with small nails. Line the new chain up with it. It will be longer, but the closest matching link, with the other end, will be behind the end of the old chain. Split it there, install, and make sure that you can shift into the two largest gears and that there is still tension while on the two smallest gears. New chains generally need new freewheels. If the new chain skips in the lower gears, an additional link can probably be removed.

Chainwheel

The primary adjustment for the chainwheel (see figures 15 and 18) is straightening. This can be done with the use of a wooden hammer, a hammer and a piece of wood, or an adjustable wrench with a rag in its jaws. By sighting on the derailleur cage, it is possible to bend the chainwheel back into alignment with the middle cog of the freewheel. Bend those alloy chainwheels very carefully. An excellent straightening can be accomplished by equalizing the distance of the teeth from a fixed point on the frame—tape a ruler to the frame so that the fractions can be read by the passing teeth.

Troubleshooting (also see *Bottom Bracket and Cranks, Chain, Derailleur—Front,* and *Pedals*):

Chain Jumps on Chainwheel. Check for a frozen link in the chain or a bent or burred tooth on the chainwheel.

Noisy Chainwheel. (See *Bottom Bracket and Cranks.*) Clean the chain and the chainwheel. Make sure the chainwheel is not bent and that it lines up with the middle cog of the freewheel.

Chain Rubs on Cage. (See *Derailleur—Front.*) Check for a bent chainwheel.

Derailleur—Front

Ideally, the cage of the front derailleur is in a plane parallel to the chainwheel, and has a curve that just clears and follows the curve of the chainwheel. When properly adjusted, the gear changes should be quick and sure, and the chain should not be thrown off the chainwheel. The cable should not be extremely slack, and the lever should be tight enough to hold it in gear.

On a front derailleur with one adjusting screw on the body (see figure 16), there are three parameters for adjustment. the adjusting screw, the cage adjusting bolt, and the cable. The adjusting screw determines the limit of outward movement of the cage. The cage adjusting bolt allows the cage to be moved inward or outward.

Two problems can be attributed to the cable: a loose cable may prevent the cage from moving inward, and a tight cable may prevent the cage from moving outward.

On the front derailleur with two adjusting screws, the additional screw determines the limit of inward movement of the cage.

Lubrication. Occasionally oil the shift lever (see figure 24), any moving parts, and pivot points with light oil, then make sure that the shift lever is tight enough to hold the derailleur in gear. You may also want to oil the arm that the cage is attached to, and the cables, in order to fight rust. It's also good to keep the cage clean, replace frayed cables, and check that the cage adjusting bolt is tight.

Troubleshooting:

Chain Thrown to Outside of Chainwheel. First of all, move the derailleur cage toward the smaller cog and screw in the outward limit adjusting screw until the cage travels only about one-fourth inch past the large chainwheel. If the adjusting screw is screwed all the way and the problem persists, bend the outer, front part of the cage slightly toward the chainwheel. If the chain is still thrown, move the cage toward the smaller chainwheel by using the cage adjusting bolt. Be careful that the chain isn't thrown off to the inside (if you have an inward limit adjusting screw, this can be compensated for). Still throws the chain? Inspect the chain for frozen links and wear, and check the chainwheel for bent teeth or crookedness.

Chain Thrown to the Inside of Chainwheel. If you have two adjusting screws, adjust the inward limit one. If you have a single adjusting screw, tighten the cable until the problem is alleviated — you might have to unscrew the outward limit adjusting screw to compensate for this. No luck? Move the cage to the outside and screw in the outward limit adjusting screw to prevent throwing the chain to the outside. If this doesn't

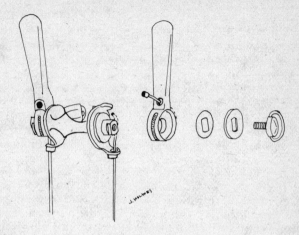

Fig. 24. The front and back gear shift levers are of the same construction. This shows an exploded view of the rear derailleur shift lever mechanism.

work, check the chain and small chainwheel for wear and tear.

Won't Go onto Small Chainwheel. Check that the cable is not too tight. If that's not it, move the cage toward the small chainwheel. If you have two adjusting screws, unscrew the inward limit screw.

Won't Go onto Large Chainwheel. Unscrew the outward limit adjusting screw. If it doesn't shift now, check to see if the cable is too loose. Still no luck? Move the cage to the outside.

Hard to Shift. Loosen the shift lever adjusting nut.

Slips Out of Gear. Tighten the shift lever adjusting nut.

Chain Hits Cage While on Large Chainwheel. Unscrew the outward limit adjusting screw, tighten cable, or move cage out.

Chain Hits Cage While on Small Chainwheel. Unscrew the inward limit adjusting screw if you have one, loosen cable, or move the cage in.

Derailleur -- Rear

Ideally, the rear derailleur should remain parallel to the chainwheel, freewheel, and the wheel. The gear change should be definite, with no slipping, and the chain should not be thrown into the spokes or the stays. The middle cog of the freewheel should line up with the large chainwheel.

The rear derailleur (see figures 25 and 26) has four parameters for adjustment: the two adjusting screws, the cable, the insertion of washers, and the spring tension for the derailleur wheels. The two adjusting screws determine the inward and outward limits of movement of the derailleur body. Two problems can be attributed to the cables: a loose cable may prevent the body from moving inward, and a tight cable may prevent the body from moving outward. The insertion of washers onto the axle will facilitate the proper centering of the wheel within the stays. The spring for the tension wheel can be tightened, but it is a rare operation on a deceptively delicate organ.

Lubrication. The pivot points, cables, and lever should be oiled regularly with light household oil. Keep the tension and jockeying wheels (see figure 27) free of gunk, and lightly oiled. Frayed cables should be replaced. It's a good idea to overhaul the rear derailleur once or twice a year by thoroughly cleaning the body and lubricating the bearings, or bushings, in the derailleur wheels. This is done by removing the tension and jockeying wheels from the cage. If the metal caps on the wheel lift off, there will be a bushing inside; if it unscrews, it'll have bearings. The bushings can be either oiled or lightly greased, while the bearings should be greased and the cones should be adjusted for minimal side play and maximum spin. Clean, oil, and reassemble. Any further disassembly should proceed only due to insatiable curiosity.

Troubleshooting:

Chain Throws Itself into Stays. First, screw down the outward limit adjusting screw. If the chain is just rubbing on the stay, insert a washer on the freewheel side of the axle. If this doesn't work, slightly tighten the cable.

Chain Throws Itself into Spokes. Screw down the inward

Fig. 25. Simplex rear derailleur showing (1) inward-limit adjusting screw, (2) outward-limit adjusting screw, (3) tension wheel spring housing, and (4) anchor bolt.

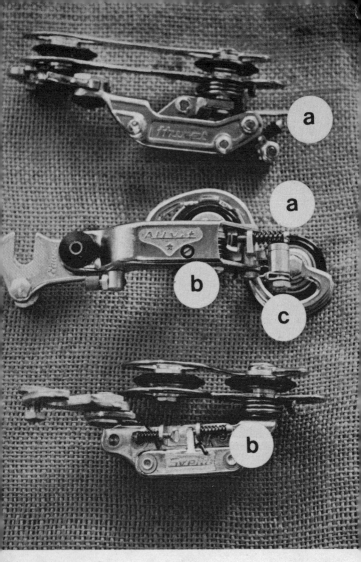

Fig. 26. Three different Huret derailleurs showing the different locations of the adjustment screws: (a) inward-limit adjusting screws, (b) outward-limit adjusting screws, and (c) anchor bolt.

Fig. 27. The tension wheel (a) and the jockeying wheel (b) should periodically be cleaned with kerosene or a light solvent; (c) marks the derailleur body and (d) the jockey-tension wheel cage.

limit adjusting screw. Still goes into the spokes? Try loosening the cable.

Chain Doesn't Move onto Small Gear. Check the outward limit adjusting screw; if it's screwed down, unscrew it, and if it's not, try loosening the cable slightly. Beyond that, oil the pivot points and check that the cage is parallel to the plane of the freewheel. The only other problem would be a loose, worn, or long chain. (See *Chain*.)

Chain Doesn't Move onto Large Chainwheel. If the inward limit adjusting screw can be unscrewed, do it. If it cannot, try tightening the cable slightly. The next step is to lubricate the pivot points and to check that the cage is parallel to the plane of the freewheel. The most extreme problem would be a short chain, in which case the jockeying wheel would bind on the large cog of the freewheel when the shift was being made (this is with the chain on the large chainwheel).

Slips Out of Gear. Tighten the adjusting nut on the shift lever.

Rough Shifting. Clean the chain and derailleur, and check for a worn, stretched chain. (See *Chain*.) Make sure the cables have the correct tension — not too slack — and the cage has the proper alignment. It's quite possible that rough gear changes or chain slippage are due to improper chain tension, which can be caused either by the chain "stretching," or by the weakening of the spring that provides the tension to the derailleur wheels. If you want to tighten the spring, there are two ways of doing it, depending on your make of derailleur: if the end of the spring is sitting in a hook on the cage, take a pair of pliers and move it to the notch that is counterclockwise to it, and, if the spring is contained in the body, take a 5 mm Allen wrench (see figure 14) and screw the lower bolt clockwise, one-eighth of a turn at a time.

Chain Skips. Check for burred teeth on the freewheel cogs or for a binding chain link. If these are in good shape, go through the procedure for *Rough Shifting.*

Fig. 28. The rear derailleur must be moved backward to allow the rear wheel to drop out.

Fig. 29. Disassembling the freewheel. The bearing retainer ring is removed in a clockwise direction.

Freewheel

Once or twice a year, the freewheel (see figure 29) should be brushed clean with kerosene or some other solvent. If the cogs grind when spun around the inside collar, you may want to soak the entire thing to clean it. Take off the rear wheel. (See figure 28.) To get the freewheel off, the freewheel remover (see figure 14) should be held in place by the quick-release bolt, and turned with a large wrench. After it's loose, remove the quick-release bolt, and turn the remover by hand. Then soak the freewheel in kerosene (spin it around a little), and after removing the excess kerosene, soak it in No. 10 machine oil. Spin off all the excess oil and reinstall. If the grinding noises persist, the freewheel needs an overhaul.

The overhaul is accomplished most easily when the freewheel is attached to the hub. The first step is to spread some newspapers and to lay the wheel flat on top of them (to catch the flying ball bearings). Then the flat ring (bearing retainer ring) with the two depressions in it has to be loosened and removed. Put an awl or punch into one of the depressions (see figure 29) and carefully tap it with a hammer, moving the ring in a clockwise direction (left-hand thread). It may take some time to get it loose, but once it's free, unscrew it by hand. This will expose the first set of bearings. (See figure 30.) Before removing the bearings, count them.

Then slowly lift the cluster and watch it rain ball bearings. Track them down along with the two or three pawls (see figure 31), which may have dropped out, and put them in a jar of kerosene. Clean everything, including the two metal shims located on the cluster body. (See figure 33.) Make sure you put the shims back before reassembling the freewheel.

The first step in reassembling the freewheel is to put high-speed bicycle grease or Lubriplate No. 110 on the top and bottom bearing races. Then replace the top bearings with the number that were removed, which should leave a space for an "extra" bearing. Turn the cluster over (the grease will hold the bearings in place) and place the rest of the bearings in the lower race, which usually leaves space for four or five "extra" bearings. (See figure 32.) Carefully set the cluster aside.

Fig. 30. Disassembling the freewheel. The first set of bearings must be counted and then removed.

Fig. 31. Disassembling the freewheel. This is the cluster body showing the pawls (a) and the springs (b).

Fig. 32. Disassembling the freewheel. Bottom view of cluster showing the grease holding the bearings in place.

This next step is the trickiest. The pawls have to be tied, in order to fit the cluster over the body, against the spring tension holding them out. (See figure 31.) Holding the pawls down, take a known length of heavy carpet thread or thin fishing line and wrap it around the cluster body so that it holds down the pawls. (See figure 33.) Keep in mind which end of the string goes over which, so when you undo it, it doesn't tie itself in knots inside your freewheel.

Gently place the bearing-ed cluster over the cluster body and screw the bearing retainer ring onto the first few threads. Slowly slide the string out, turning the cluster a little to help free the string. If you end up with the same length of string that you started with, you are a success. If not, you can start over.

Fig. 33. Black line extending from the number 1 points to a cluster body holding shims. The cluster's pawls, springlike mechanisms, are held in place by heavy string wrapped around them in the cluster body.

Troubleshooting:

Grinding Noises from the Freewheel. Clean the chain, chain-wheel, and freewheel. If this doesn't work, go through the lubricating procedure. And if it still persists, go through the overhaul procedure.

Everything Turns but the Rear Wheel. Overhaul the freewheel, looking for jammed pawls.

Headset

Ideally, when the bike is off the ground, the headset (see figure 34) should move with such ease that the slightest nudge on the front wheel should move it to its fullest extent, in either direction. Yet, there should not be any horizontal or vertical play in the forks—this can be treated as a typical cone-bearing adjustment.

Lubricating. Once or twice a year, the headset should be re-greased. To do this, first disconnect the brake (see figure 35) and then remove the handlebars and front wheel. Remove the locknut and washer. (See figure 34.) By slowly unscrewing the top race, the bottom bearing should come into view. Stop and see if they are loose or in a retainer ring. If they are in a retainer ring, there's no problem; hold the fork in the front tube and see if the top bearings are in a retainer ring. If the bottom bearings are loose, hold a bag or some suitable catching device under the lower race, and continue to unscrew the top race. Most of the bearings should fall out, and those that don't can be prodded out. Count these bearings for future reference, then push the forks back into the front tube and remove the top race. If the top bearings are loose but look secure, carefully pull the forks out, put your hand beneath the tube, and push the bearings through. If they don't look secure, use the catching device. Count them.

Clean all the parts and start to reassemble the headset. If the bearings were loose, the following procedure may help you keep track of them. Grease the race on the forks and the top race on the front tube. Then, with half of the bearings in your hand, push the forks into the tube, set the top bearings, and screw the locknut onto the first few threads. Let the forks drop and then set the bottom bearings in the exposed race. Carefully

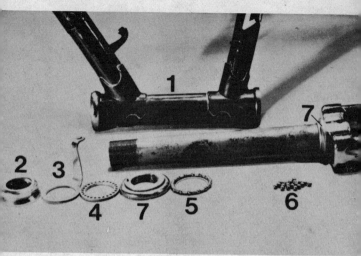

Fig. 34. Exploded view of the headset where the front fork assembly fits into the frame. Parts are: (1) head tube of the frame, (2) locknut, (3) brake cable holder, (4) washer, (5) top bearings in the retainer ring, (6) loose bottom bearings, and (7) top and bottom races.

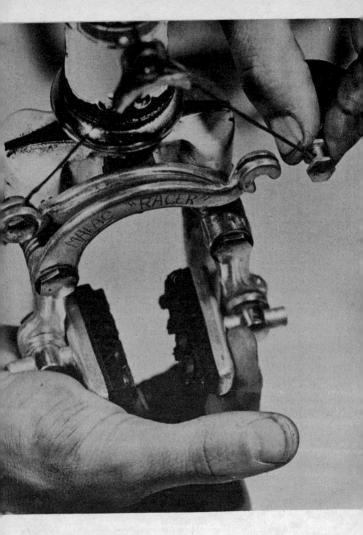

Fig. 35. Proper brake adjustment is attained by tightening the pads to the point where it is difficult to remove the wheel without unhitching the brake cable. To unhitch the cable, squeeze the pads against the rim and slip out the yoke anchor.

push the forks back into the front tube and tighten the top race. The top race acts as an adjustable cone, so screw it down until there is no side or vertical play, but not so tight that there isn't free swing. Put the washer on, tighten the locknut, and re-test the adjustment.

Troubleshooting:

Front End Chatter. Tighten the race on the headset, but make sure it still swings easily. If it wasn't loose, check for side play in the front wheel (see *Hubs*), and for an out-of-round rim.

Difficult Steering. This problem is most likely due to a tight or dirty headset. Try loosening it first, and check for grinding noises. If the headset cannot be adjusted right, go through the lubrication procedure and check for deformed bearings and races.

Hubs

The hubs have a typical cone-bearing relationship (see figure 36), which should be adjusted tight enough to eliminate side play and loose enough to facilitate free rotation. (See figure 37.) A perfectly adjusted wheel will behave like a pendulum, where the valve stem is the weight.

Lubrication. The hubs should be greased about two times a year, depending on how much you use your bike. To disassemble the hub, remove the locknut and cone from one end of the axle (if you don't want to remove the freewheel, take off the cone opposite the freewheel). Catch, count, and inspect the bearings as you pull out the axle. Pitted or grooved cones should be replaced. The dust caps on the hub can be pried off and the entire hub, axle, bearings, cones, and quick-release bolt should be cleaned – the more surgically, the better.

In the reassembly procedure, if you removed the dust caps, replace them first. Then blow into the hub to remove any metal shavings that might have been produced when replacing the dust caps. Put a light to moderate layer of grease on the hub race and the cone. Set half of the bearings, insert the axle, hold the opposite end of the axle, and flip the wheel. Grease this side and continue reassembling. The cones should be adjusted as cited above.

Troubleshooting:

Wheel Doesn't Spin Freely. Check the cone adjustment. If the cones cannot be loosened to give free rotation because of the side-to-side movement, the hubs have to be relubricated.

Wheel Sounds Gritty. Take the axle in both hands, and with your third hand, give the wheel a spin. Grit and grime can be felt through the axle. If the grit is in the hubs, regrease them.

Wobbly Wheel. Try tightening the cones if there is any side-to-side movement. Check for a crooked rim. (See *Rims.*)

Fig. 36. An exploded view of a wheel hub (construction is the same on both wheels) showing: (1) the quick-release skewer rod, (2) axle, (3) loose wheel bearings, (4) cone, (5) washer, and (6) locknut. This is a cone-bearing relationship found in virtually all bicycles.

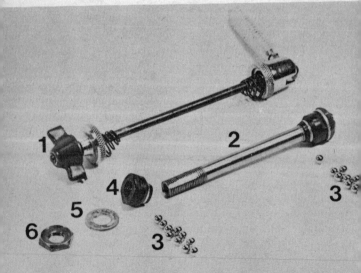

Fig. 37. Adjustment of cones requires both wrenches be brought together in one quick movement, tightening the locknut against the cone.

Pedals

Pedals are set up with a cone-bearing relationship. If the dust cap can be removed, the cone can generally be adjusted to eliminate side play and to maximize for spin.

Lubrication. Pedals should be regreased once or twice a year (pedals without adjustable cones should be oiled frequently). The right pedal has conventional threads, but the left pedal has left-hand threads (unscrew clockwise). After taking the pedals off the cranks, remove the dust cap, the locknut, the adjustable cone, and the bearings. (See figure 38.) Count the bearings and put them aside (there usually are fewer outside than inside bearings). Then pull the axle out of the pedal shaft, remove, count, and inspect the bearings, and put them aside. Clean all the parts, lightly grease the cones and races, and reassemble. Then adjust the cones as mentioned above.

Troubleshooting:

Pedal Too Loose or Tight. Remove the dust cap and adjust the cone for minimal side play and maximum spin. If the pedal remains tight, regrease it and check for a bent axle.

Squeaky Pedal. Remove the dust cap and shoot some oil around the cone, trying to work it into the inside bearings as well. If that doesn't work, try loosening the cone slightly. The last step is to regrease the pedal and to check for a bent axle.

Rims and Spokes

Along with the hub, the rims and spokes are also known as the wheel. The rim is held planar by the tension of the spokes.

Troubleshooting:

Dings. These small outcroppings in the rim, usually caused by hitting rocks and potholes, can be repaired with a pair of vise grips. By slowly closing the gap between the jaws, in successive "clamps," the rim will approach its original smoothness. Small indentations cause fewer problems than small outcroppings.

Bent Rim. If your rim is bent or wobbly, it can be straightened by the proper tuning of the spokes. Hold a crayon near the rim

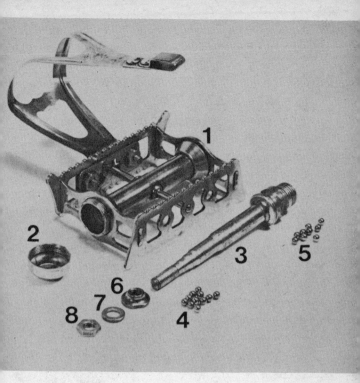

Fig. 38. An exploded view of a pedal, showing: (1) the pedal, (2) dust cap, (3) pedal axle, (4) and (5) pedal bearings, (6) adjustable cone, (7) washer, and (8) locknut.

and spin the wheel. This will mark the "high" and "low" points along the rim. To straighten, loosen the spokes coming from the marked side of the hub, and tighten the spokes on the other side. It's important that the spokes not be too tight or too loose. If the spokes on the "high" side of the hub are already loose but those on the opposite side are tight, move down four spokes (if the spokes are arranged in series of four) both ways and loosen the one on the marked side and tighten the one on the other side. Turn the spokes a one-quarter turn at a time and sight the distance of the brake pads to the rim to check on how you are doing.

To tighten a spoke, from the top view, take the spoke wrench (see figure 14) and turn the nipple clockwise, and to loosen turn it counterclockwise (see figure 39). It's important to note that the "outside" spokes, or the ones with the spoke head facing toward the center, will be more effective in moving the rim a large distance than the "inside" spokes. And it's important to notice that the rear wheel is dished, or flatter, on its freewheel side.

Out-of-Round Wheel. Tuning the spokes to correct for a slightly out-of-round wheel is difficult, so live with it, and replace it or rebuild it when it becomes intolerable.

Replacing Spokes. Spokes are generally laced in series of four, so, by looking at the fourth spoke from the broken one, you'll be able to determine how the new one should be laced. It's often possible to replace the spoke nipple without removing the tire from the rim. Just deflate the tire and push it to one side. The beveled side of the spoke hole, in the hub, is not for the spoke head, but to relieve the strain on the bending spoke.

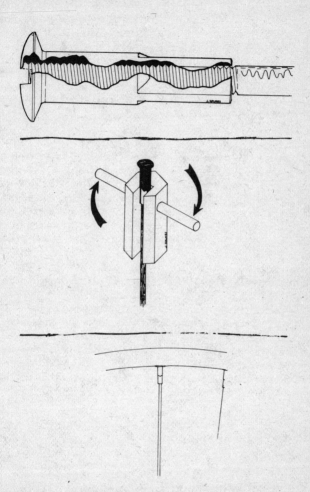

Fig. 39. Three views of the spoke and the spoke nipple. The top view shows a cutaway closeup of the nipple threaded onto the spoke. The middle view shows a spoke wrench tightening the apparatus by turning clockwise on the nipple where it protrudes from the rim, as shown in the bottom view.

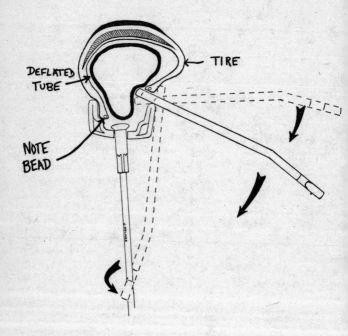

Fig. 40. To remove a clincher tire from its lipped rim, deflate the tube and pry up the tire's bead with a tire iron or a dull, broad screwdriver.

Tires

Fixing flats on clinchers or tubular tires (sew-ups) is a straightforward operation. The leak has to be located, exposed, patched, and, most importantly, the cause has to be determined. There are a few helpful hints to make the procedure swift.

Removal. The fewer tools used in the removal of a clincher tire, the fewer your chances of causing another puncture. If the tire bead cannot be removed from the rim by hand, use tire irons or dull, broad screwdrivers. Often, when the puncture is obvious, the tire can be repaired without removing the wheel. Just pull a small section of the bead off the rim and pull out the tube. (See figure 40.) Inflate, confirm, and mark the leak. Then patch it, and put the tire back on the rim. You may want to dust the patch with talcum to prevent its sticking to the tire casing.

If the leak isn't obvious on your clincher, check the valve with a little spit — a loose valve won't hold air, so tighten it. If it's not the valve, remove the bead on one side of the rim, and pull most of the tube out, leaving the valve stem in place. Inflate, locate the leak, mark it, and patch. If you still can't find the puncture, take the entire tube out, inflate it, and dunk it in water.

On tubular tires (sew-ups), it is always best, but not always possible, to find the leak when the tire is still on the rim. Inflate it and turn it through a water bath. Then mark it. To remove a tubular, just roll the portion of the tire, opposite the valve, off the rim — the rest comes easy.

Repair. Clincher tires have a different patch kit than tubulars, but the patching process is the same. Roughen the surface around the puncture and apply a thin layer of glue, the same size as the patch. When the glue loses its shine, take the backing off the patch and press it onto the glue. When the patch has set, it's a good idea to dust it with talcum. At this point, it is of paramount importance to determine the cause of the puncture, be it glass, tacks, nails, wire, or whatever.

The problem with tubular tires is getting to the right portion of the tube. If the leak is obvious, pull off about six inches of the tape that covers the stitches. (See figure 41.) Mark every five opposing thread holes with a pencil (this aids in resewing the tire), and cut about two inches of the stitching. Be careful, there's a tube under there. Below the stitching, there will be a chafing tape, which will have to be moved aside. Pull a couple of inches of the tube through the hole, slightly inflate the tire, and locate the leak. Go through the patching procedure. If you can't find the leak, immerse the tire, and notice which direction the bubbles come from the casing — cut that way.

If the leak couldn't be located while the tire was on the rim, take it off, inflate it, and put it through some water. Air will escape from the casing at the valve, but this is not necessarily the location of the puncture. Look carefully.

When resewing the tubular tire, it's important to put the thread through the same holes they were in before, and to sew with even tension on each stitch. If you don't do this, the tire may bulge or develop an S-turn in the tire tread — either of which will weaken the tire. The final procedures are to glue the tape back on and to glue the tire onto the rim. (If the glue on the rim is tacky, don't mess it up with more glue. If there is a lot of glue on the rim, it can be made tacky with white gas.) Put the valve in the rim, stretch the tire, and start fitting it to the rim. Practice makes perfect.

Hints. If you cut the sidewall on a tubular tire, don't throw it away — it may be repairable. After fixing the tube, put a few darning stitches in the sidewall, pulling the wound closed. Cut a patch from thin cardboard, glue it to the inside of the casing, and dust it with talcum. With luck, the tire will be usable and you'll have saved some dollars.

If you have a bad valve, the tube can be salvaged. First, check the valve — if it has a locknut at its base, it can be recovered. Cut that section of the tube out, unscrew the nut, remove the washer (seal), and pull the stem out from beneath. To make a new one, cut the nonfunctional valve from the tube and patch the hole. Cut a small hole at least six inches from the patch and work the bottom of the stem into the tube. Take a patch and punch a hole in the center (slightly smaller than the diameter of the valve) and glue it to the tube. Put the washer

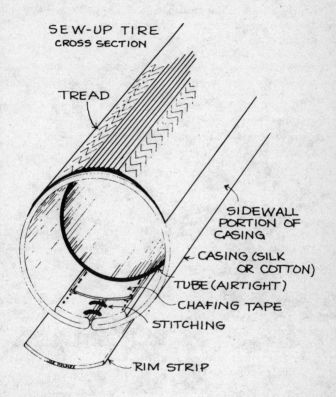

SEW-UP TIRE
CROSS SECTION

TREAD

SIDEWALL
PORTION OF
CASING

CASING (SILK
OR COTTON)

TUBE (AIRTIGHT)

CHAFING TAPE

STITCHING

RIM STRIP

Fig. 41. The sew-up (or tubular) tire. Note how the tire casing is sewed
entirely around the tire's inner tube. Repairs on sew-ups are tricky
but with practice and care easily done.

on and screw the locknut down tight. This will save you money, but it takes time.

The tubes also come in handy as giant rubber bands, shock cords, covers for case-hardened chains, exercisers, and slingshots.

FACTS ABOUT MY BIKE

GENERAL:

Make_____ Model_____ Serial No._____

Size of frame_____

Place purchased_____ Date purchased_____

Registration or license no._____

EQUIPMENT:

Tire size_____

Brakes_____

Gearing brand_____ Front teeth_____ Rear teeth_____

_____   _____

_____

_____

_____

_____

Bearings

   Front wheel (one side)   _____

   Rear wheel (one side)   _____

   Bottom bracket (one side)_____

   Pedals inside   _____

         outside_____

Headset_____

6 Health and Safety

A healthy person is a safe person. Safety is healthy for all persons. Danger is bad, as is ill-health. That goes for everybody.

Bicycles are neither safe nor dangerous. They are neither healthy nor unhealthy. Bicycles are.

People and bicycles often go together. People can go without bicycles, but bicycles cannot go without people. There is no will involved.

If people and bicycles often go together, to wherever, then they should, in combination, produce a safe, healthy, i.e., good result rather than a dangerous, unhealthy, i.e., bad result. Otherwise, the two should never go together, even just for a ride around the block. We—people, that is—all know how innocent acts can result in tragedy.

So, in order to produce a good rather than bad effect when combining with a bicycle, one should be well informed. Information, though in and of itself not an absolute preventative, is most certainly a prophylactic.

The septuagenarian doctor had retired to a small practice in a country town a few hours' drive from the city. There, he could see patients at his leisure and spend many hours at his favorite pastime, bicycling. At the request of some old friends, he agreed to come to the local college once a semester to give a lecture on health and bicycling. It was an easy task actually, since the data was extremely clear and simple and he had the material virtually memorized. On the morning of his lecture, the city sky was clear and he enjoyed his drive to the campus even though he knew that by the time class began, the air would be gray and gloomy.

The 9:00 o'clock lecture opened quite simply:

"The average American is a cigarette smoker, which is bad enough," the doctor said. "He complicates matters by tending to be underexercised and tension ridden. These conditions, in combination, make a person a ripe candidate for heart disease, an affliction that hits men earlier in life than women. The dangers, however, are not limited to either sex.

"When a person fails to exercise, his heart muscle shrinks. It beats less regularly, blood vessels narrow, the amount of protein in muscles decreases, and the body uses oxygen in an inefficient and wasteful manner. Some studies have shown a relationship in old people between senility and the body's diminishing ability to transfer oxygen to its various parts, particularly the brain.

"In a well-exercised body, high blood pressure is often decreased, lungs fill to greater capacity, and there is usually a lower blood level of fats, cholesterol, and other fat fractions of the blood. These blood fats are suspected of participating in causing heart disease — because they deposit themselves in the walls of the heart, restricting the blood supply to the heart itself. Exercise decreases the amount of these substances but the decrease is temporary. Thus the necessity for regular exercise."

The hours changed but the lecture stayed the same. By 11:15 the gray tint had the sky fully in its grip. In between the middle of his sentences the doctor would cough, a light rasp that indicated mild irritation.

"Among people under sixty-five, there are more than 250,000 deaths a year that are in some way related to cardiovascular diseases. Many of them are caused by the heart being forced to overwork. Studies have shown that 30 percent of blood circulation is carried on by leg muscles when a person is walking about — or riding.

"Vigorous leg muscle exercise is probably one of the best methods" — the doctor paused to cough several times in rapid succession — "to keep the veins clear and to prevent the formation of blood clots. Walking, dancing, tennis, swimming, golf when played without the benefit of a cart, are all excellent forms of exercise."

"Dr. Paul Dudley White, a heart specialist who attended the late President Dwight Eisenhower, has said, 'The leg muscles are an important and unappreciated accessory pumping mechanism to assist our hearts physically. Healthy fatigue of the big muscle is the best antidote known to man for nervous stress, far better than the use of the thousand and one tranquilizers and sedatives to which American people have become addicted.'

"In addition to improving the legs and the heart, cycling is one of the most complete forms of exercise, extending its benefits to arm, shoulder, back, abdominal and diaphragmatic muscles. The diaphragm operates in our chest like a suction pump, enhancing blood return to the heart.

"A Washington, D.C., psychiatrist, Claire Cobb, suffered two slipped cervical disks in her back as the result of an automobile accident a few years ago. On the advice of her neurologist, she took up bicycling and soon reported that as long as she rides some sixty miles a week, she doesn't suffer any back pains. If she misses a day because of the weather, she hurts. Of course, people can also ride indoor bicycle exercisers to prevent cloudy days from interrupting their exercise schedules.

"A British physician, Dr. Christopher Woodward, fills out the list of medical bicycle benefits. Cycles, the good doctor says, are used in the physiotherapy departments of every hospital. After major operations they are often used to recover muscle tone faster and more effectively than any other method. They are used in the after-treatment of several kinds of arm and leg fractures. It is far better for the patient to exercise his own limbs rather than have them exercised for him by massage, electrical or short-wave diathermy.

"A vast group of rheumatic and arthritic complaints also come within the range of illnesses for which cycling can be an essential part of the treatment. By toning up the right set of muscles, pedaling can reduce the risk of hernia and other forms of rupture or reduce the risk of slipped disks in the back. And finally, Dr. Woodward adds, mothers-to-be can safely continue to cycle almost to the end of their pregnancies."

By 1:30, in the middle of his third lecture, the gray in the sky had thickened and the doctor was using lozenges to soothe the irritation in his throat. He continued:

"Three years ago, Dr. Harry Bass, of Boston's Peter Brigham Hospital, directed patients with emphysema to start riding bicycles. Emphysema is a condition of the lungs that afflicts more than four hundred thousand Americans and causes about twenty thousand deaths in this country each year."

The doctor was silent for a moment, and noticed that two of the students were using eyedrops to still the mild burning sensation in their eyes that the acrid smog had caused. He also couldn't help noticing the increase in the number of people coughing when compared to the morning class.

"Under a research program begun a year before and reported in *Medical World News,* Dr. Bass had fourteen men and women, all afflicted with moderate to severe emphysema, riding bicycles under close supervision. After eighteen weeks every patient was leading a more active life. 'Before the study,' Dr. Bass said at the time, 'many of the patients were immobilized to such an extent that they were confined to the house. Now they are out and back to work. One physician in the test group has resumed his practice. All of the patients feel better, do a lot more, and lead a better life in general.'

"Dr. Bass also noted that, after twelve weeks of the program, the patients showed several other signs of improved health. Pulse rates decreased, both at rest and under a given exercise load, heart functioning was more efficient, work less exhausting, and they built up muscles."

In between classes, the doctor glanced out the window. He was not surprised to find an almost total lack of visibility. Under the growing pall, he returned to his classroom for his final lecture of the day.

"I don't know how many of you noted the story in *Life* magazine, toward the end of 1971, which told about a country school football team arriving in New Jersey for a game. The whole team was taken ill and the source of their sickness was traced to air pollution, a condition that the boys weren't ready for since they were used to relatively clean country air. In Los Angeles, for the past several years, there have been frequent smog alerts and schoolchildren are not allowed to play in the yard for fear that their lungs will take in too many poisons.

"It seems futile to me to prevent children from playing in a school yard if they are only going to ride their bicycles home after school, a time of day when the smog is thickest. Of all the rhythmic forms of exercise, I recommend bicycling, of course, because it is so complete. It offers greater social contact—and even for a man in his seventies, social contact is important," he said, with a flicker of a smile, "and it affords a communion with the outdoors that can only be matched by hiking.

"But it is becoming increasingly impossible to talk about bicycling and health without talking about air pollution and health. I wonder if some of Dr. Bass's emphysema patients could have survived that," he said, pointing out the window.

"This is my last lecture today and I haven't made these comments to the other classes. I hope your professor will pass them on." The professor nodded. "It is getting increasingly difficult to lead a private life nowadays," were the doctor's closing remarks. "The world has many devious ways of bringing its problems to your door. And pollution respects no boundaries and knows no real limits. What service will bicycle paths be if it is unsafe to vigorously breathe the air?"

The preceding discussion was simplistic and to the point as is most of the material available on the health benefits of bicycling. Very little hard data is available to back up claims, but there appears to be, among doctors who have looked into the matter, an almost total consensus that bicycling health benefits are numerous and potent.

The strong of body and heart resist colds, virus infections, pneumonia, many abdominal complaints, and a host of other ailments far better than the average person. Psychological well-being is considered to have a strong positive effect on physical well-being and the relaxation brought about by exercise is repeatedly noted as a benefit of two-wheel transportation.

When compared to automobiles in terms of mechanical safety, the bicycle outranks the car so much that there isn't really a contest, though a recent addition to bicycle styles is helping to close that gap. Initial studies of bicycles characterized the machine's safety as unequaled. In a 1969 National

Safety Council research report, a study of more than four thousand bicycle accidents revealed that only thirty-three indicated that equipment failure was a contributing factor and of those thirty-three, two-thirds of the failures were a result of improper maintenance.

That particular report may have been deficient, however, since bicycling is a somewhat risky business accounting for more than one million injuries annually, including 120,000 fractures, 60,000 concussions, and 800 deaths resulting primarily from collisions with automobiles.

And adding remarkably to those statistics is a recently introduced new style characterized by high, wide handlebars, a short wheelbase, small wheel size, especially in the front, and elongated seats. Common additional features include two fixtures placed about the seat, a tall, chrome "sissy" bar behind and a console gear shift mounted on a crossbar directly in front. In 1968, *Consumer Bulletin* noted that these models were said to account for 60 percent of the industry's sales.

Two years before, a *Newsweek* article drew attention to the daredevil ambiance that accompanies the Stingray, the compact, lightweight bike that usually has only twenty-inch wheels and which then accounted for more than 90 percent of all California sales. *Newsweek* wrote:

> The Stingray's appeal lies in its power to make a seven-year-old come on like Steve McQueen aboard his Triumph. The low center of gravity permits him to perform such stunts as "wheelies" (pulling up on the handlebars, leaning back and riding briefly on the rear wheels only) and "jumpies" (jamming on the brakes so that the bike takes off and flies for as much as six feet). Stingray owners also borrow from the auto cultists. In California, the kids are spraying their bike frames with "diamond flake" paint and putting wildly hued slipcovers over the saddles. And imitating the drag strip crowd, they are installing treadless tires called "racing slicks" on the rear wheels for faster starts.

By 1971, advertising departments had made a practice of associating daredevil behavior with this model bicycle, and the Stingray was joined by the Beast, the Screamer, and the Barracuda. Companies were also putting out booklets that were alleged to deal with safety education but which emphasized stunt riding.

According to Dr. Allan B. Coleman, chairman of the Committee on Accident Prevention of the American Academy of Pediatrics, these styles "are causing undue numbers of cheek injuries," a relatively mild complaint when compared with a study by Dr. T. R. Howell, who found an "epidemic of injuries to the skull and face, among children using the bicycles."

A study made by the National Safety Council agreed with the doctors, stating that the new bike styles cause proportionately more injuries than the traditional designs.

The bicycles were sent to the Cornell Aeronautical Laboratory for design analysis. The report concluded that "the shorter wheelbase and smaller wheel size are detrimental to both lateral and vertical plane stability," meaning that the bike's design not only makes it more difficult to ride but also more susceptible to pitch forward in a cartwheel if it strikes an obstacle or drops into a rut.

There are other unnecessary dangers. Since the stick shift on the crossbar protrudes upward like a stake, there is a marked risk of injury to the rider's genitals. His steering ability is diminished by having to take a hand off the handlebars when shifting. There are also increased possibilities of frame or fork failures. The sissy bar and the elongated seat encourage trick riding. And the National Safety Commission found the seat also promotes double riding, a significant cause of accidents in poorer neighborhoods, leaving the bike not only risky but racist.

The Bicycle Manufacturers Association, affiliated with the Bicycle Institute of America, has developed standards for safety, and to be certified by the BMA, something to watch for when buying a bicycle, all equipment must meet their requirements.

Brakes

From a speed of fifteen miles per hour, a bicycle will stop in a distance of thirty feet or less for at least twenty-six consecutive stops. At a wheel speed of two hundred revolutions per minute, coaster brakes must provide 1.2 horsepower of stopping force when a pressure of twenty pound-feet of torque is applied. The test of coaster brakes is always conducted after twenty-five stops are made at two-minute intervals with twelve pound-feet of pressure applied, giving the brakes opportunity to reveal mechanical weaknesses under stress. With hand brakes, the distance from the brake lever's center to the opposite gripping surface must not be more than three inches. Shoes must assure retention of the brake blocks. With an axle load of fifty pounds and maximum recommended tire pressure, there must be a minimum of thirty pounds of retarding force exerted before any skidding begins.

Frame Load Carrying Ability

No rupture, breakage, or hazard-producing distortion can occur with less than a load of 300 pounds on the saddle or 225 pounds on tandems (multiple-seat bikes). Bikes also must support 300 pounds of pressure on the center of a pedal at its lowest position with 100 pounds on the opposing pedal. Tandems: 225 pounds on the low pedal, 75 pounds on its opposite. Hand grips are expected to withstand 50 pounds of pressure on single bikes and 37.5 on tandems.

Single bikes are expected to hold a total load of 800 pounds, tandems 1,200, with loads supported at the rear axle and lower end of the head tube. The distortion of the bicycle's permanent set, measured at the seat tube on a line between the rear axle and the bottom of the seat tube, shall not exceed one-half inch with maximum loading. No fracture, failure, or fork-setting distortion of more than three-quarters of an inch is tolerated with loads of less than 200 pounds perpendicularly applied to the fork axis, or after the five impacts of twenty-five pounds coupled with a seventy-five pound preload.

Handlebars

Handlebars must be fourteen to twenty-eight inches wide and no higher than sixteen inches above the saddle. Pressure is measured in two areas, the bars and stem and the stem and fork, since leverage actually extends all the way down the wheel. With pressure being applied clockwise and counterclockwise, and seventy-five pound-feet of torque being exerted at the grips, no more than two degrees of slippage is allowed of the handlebars and stem. With thirty-five pound-feet of torque being exerted at the grips, no more than two degrees of slippage is tolerated between the stem and fork.

Structural Integrity

With tires inflated to their maximum recommended pressure and the bicycle loaded to 150 pounds and driven at fifteen miles per hour for three hours, the wheels are then subjected to impact from one-half-inch-high, two-inch-wide cleats with flattened edges, fastened one foot apart on a rotating drum. No breakdown of tire walls resulting in pressure loss or removal of the tire from the rim may occur.

The BMA test places the bicycle on two rotating drums, thirty inches in diameter, each fitted with the cleats used in the safety tests. The drums rotate out of phase at five miles per hour for one hour with a two hundred-pound live load (pity the man with that job), the crank axle loaded to eighty pounds, the seat loaded to eighty pounds, the head tube to thirty pounds, and an extra ten pounds of load attachments. No component breakage or deformation resulting in hazard to the riders is permitted under those conditions.

Miscellaneous

Wheels and forks must be factory assembled with bearings properly adjusted and front axle nuts tightened to twelve pound-feet of torque and rear nuts to twenty pound-feet. Pedals must clear the ground by at least three and one-half inches and in a horizontal position to the front, must clear the wheel or fender by a minimum of three inches. Rear red reflectors are expected to meet the same standards as automobiles, as defined by the Society of Automotive Engineers. Furthermore, in a darkness broken only by two headlights on low beam, set at a distance of three hundred feet, and with an observer in a car's driver's seat, the rear reflectors and white pedal reflector must be visible. With the bicycle rotated a full 360 degrees, additional reflective material must be seen from the front and sides.

Special considerations should be made when purchasing bicycles for children. The derailleur-type gear, in which the mechanism is exposed and operated by "derailing" the chain from one set of gears to another, is not particularly well suited for youngsters because it gets out of adjustment and alignment too easily with the rigorous use/abuse children inflict on their toys.

The National Safety Council has pointed out that a bicycle's size in relation to its rider is of paramount safety importance. An adult naturally picks a style that fits him, but if he is buying for someone else, he often neglects that criteria. The NSC has found a high incidence of accidents involving children riding bikes too large for them.

Most lists of road rules for pedalers are so simplistic that they tend to be vaguely insulting to anyone possessing a modicum of intelligence. They frequently include reminders to observe traffic regulations, not to hitch onto other vehicles, to listen for traffic approaching from out of your line of vision, not to weave in and out of traffic, to watch other traffic, to use hand signals, to use reflectors at night, and other pappy principles.

On occasion an intelligent list is compiled. Ralph W. Galen, president of the League of American Wheelmen, suggests:

1. Never raise the stem of the handlebars to the extent that the split in the stem can be seen. A broken stem will leave the rider in a helpless condition.

2. When riding down a steep hill at high speed, keep the pedals horizontal to the ground and press your knees against the top bar. This will serve to dampen any vibration and/or whip that might be set up in the frame. Once a vibration is set up, it is almost impossible to stop it without either coming to a complete stop or by falling.

3. Check the quick-release levers before going on a ride or trip. A quick-release lever can become caught on another bicycle and the wheel loosened without the rider becoming aware of this condition until an emergency situation sets in.

4. Keep your equipment clean and in good condition. Regu-

lar care will not only keep your equipment looking new longer but will keep it running in better condition.

5. Once a wheel has been trued or the spokes adjusted following an accident or spoke replacement, *always* remove the tire to be certain that no spokes are protruding beyond the nipple head. A tube puncture from an extended spoke can not only be a nuisance but can also be the source of a serious accident.

Revolution

7 Politics

Earlier in this book, we discussed bicycle mechanics. Now, we'll discuss political mechanics. Since you've no doubt familiarized yourself with certain esoteric cycle terminology, you'll find it easy to apply your newfound knowledge to any situation. Let us proceed.

Many politicians are cranks. Their executive decisions seldom have any bearing on environmental problems, yet they like to keep the ball rolling. In order to wrench a statement from them, one almost has to chain them to a track or else they get derailed. The purpose of this chapter is to show you how to keep them in one gear rather than have them speed off in ten different directions when a particular problem arises and you have a solution.

If people have been slow to realize the bicycle's full potential as a means of transportation, the government has been slower. It is ironic that cyclists, riding a nonpolluting machine, must endure the arrogant flatulence of a machine that is inherently dirty, yet is subsidized by the same government that wants to fight the pollution problem. Bicycling, like pollution, started out as a harmless political issue—politicians bicycled around with big grins, making lame statements about health, fresh air, and exercise. But lately bicycling has developed heavy implications for transportation and land use. Cycling could radically alter concepts of city planning and development if the people begin to think bicycle instead of car. We will discuss various ways to achieve these changes, first at various levels of bureaucracy and then by direct action.

One of America's basic assumptions equates the automobile with transportation. City planners have tried to accommodate the automobile, but as the number of cars increases, the plans become less efficient. With the nation tooled up for automobiles, legislators find it easy to favor auto transport through indirect subsidies. With the promise of 90 percent funding from the Federal Highway Trust Fund, city planners and developers can hardly afford to pass up the chance for more roads, and, since World War II, the number of fume-spewing automobiles using these roads has increased: In effect, this policy has created a government subsidy to the car and to the automobile industry. In the face of dire auto pollution, city people are hard pressed to find immediate transportation alternatives while suburbia, the child of the automobile, cannot operate without it.

On May 8, 1971, a number of congressmen gathered for a brief ride around the Capitol to celebrate National Bikecology Day. It was pleasant and painless, and everyone's picture made the papers. Few of these men, however, were around to help get bike racks in the House garage to aid the growing number of Capitol Hill staffers who bike to work. Recently, the old bike tune has changed somewhat as congressmen realize that more than eighty million American cyclists aren't playing with a toy, but are using a form of transportation that could be the basis of the cheapest and most efficient in-city transportation system ever devised. To make this transportation system a reality, definite changes must take place to enable the cyclist safe, easy travel in the city streets.

The most important thing to do to promote change in transportation modes is to determine exactly who makes the decisions and who supplies the money to implement these decisions. To do this you must do research into the workings of the local, county, and federal government agencies that are concerned with bicycling.

On the municipal level, get to know the traffic and highway engineers in your town. Familiarize yourself with their publications. If you don't understand them, get someone to help you go through them so that you will be able to look at situations from the point of view of the traffic engineer. Know who your park and recreation people are and what their future plans are. Find out what they have done and what they haven't done. Park and planning people are usually the last people on the money totem pole, so be aware of their limitations.

Find out who the road people are on the county level and what long-term plans they have for the area. Where will the new roads go in your area? What effect will they have on population centers? Where is the money in the area and who controls it?

On the state level, many of the programs may already be so diffused that it may be difficult to zero in on specific parts of agencies. Politicians have an enormous amount of power to make things happen on the state level. If possible, you should go to the state capital to visit directly with your state representative and the appropriate committees that are concerned with transportation. Prepare yourself before you go. Politicians see thousands of people and they don't have a lot of time, so have your questions or proposal ready before you go to see them.

Use the charts on pages 136–137 to list the names and the phone numbers of all these people in one place.

Once you have an idea of what's going on, you should come up with a firm proposal that you can offer the bureaucrats. The most important part of the proposal as far as the bureaucrats are concerned is how much it will cost. The clearer and cheaper the proposal, the easier it will be to get it implemented. Your proposal can take any of the following general forms.

Bike Lanes. This is a portion of streets that is reserved exclusively for bicycles. It can require as little as five feet of curb lane or can use an entire car lane. These lanes should be marked clearly, forbidden to cars, and should connect with other transportation systems, places of work, commercial areas, and recreational areas. Routes can be determined by interested cyclists, a bike poll, or by city layout. These bike lanes should link up with bike paths that bypass difficult highway and freeway interchanges and should be a part of an integrated transportation system that presents a safe place to cycle, encouraging more people to ride, and making cities quieter, cleaner, and less congested.

Bike Paths. These are paved or tightly compacted trails for bicycles. They are expensive and take time to construct. They should be constructed only where mixing bikes and high-speed cars would be foolhardy, and their construction, when possible, should be on existing, abandoned roads. More pavement is not needed, even for bikes. To those pushing for bike paths in

HANDY BUREAUCRAT DIRECTORY

LOCAL	NAME	PHONE
Traffic Dept. Head	_____	_____
Traffic Planners, Engineers, Contacts	_____	_____
	_____	_____
Parks and Recreation People	_____	_____
Pertinent Elected Officials	_____	_____
	_____	_____
	_____	_____
	_____	_____

COUNTY		
Highway Dept. Head	_____	_____
Recreation and Parks	_____	_____
County Planners	_____	_____
Pertinent Elected Officials	_____	_____

HANDY BUREAUCRAT DIRECTORY

STATE	NAME	PHONE
State Highway	_____	_____
Recreation and Parks	_____	_____
State Planners	_____	_____
Pertinent Elected Officials *State Reps*	_____	_____
Committee	_____	_____
	_____	_____
Committee	_____	_____
Governor	_____	_____
	_____	_____

NATIONAL		
Dept. of Transportation	_____	_____
Dept. of Interior	_____	_____
Dept. of HUD	_____	_____
Pertinent Elected Officials	_____	_____

many of our urban areas, this note of caution: once a bike path is built, even if it goes nowhere, city and road officials may demand that cyclists use the path and get off the road. A bike path, especially a poorly located or incomplete one, should never serve as an excuse to get the cyclist off a road to which he has as much right as the motorist. Officials use many tactics in sweeping the way clear for motor vehicles under the guise of protection for the cyclist. And protect you they will . . . right out of existence.

Bikeways. This term is the cause of more confusion than any other. As used by the Bicycle Institute of America, a primary promoter of the bikeway program, it seems to refer to ordinary city streets marked with signs designating them as bikeways. There is no separation of the cyclist and motorist. Essentially there is nothing new here at all; it is the same road that it always is with the same drivers.

Bike Racks. Bike lanes, bike paths, or even bikeways are useless unless there is a safe, inexpensive place to put the bike once the cyclist arrives at his destination. Bike racks must be provided if the bicycling movement is to continue rolling. Special municipal parking lots for bikes must be constructed. Car parking lots can be available to cyclists for a nominal charge. Private businessmen should be encouraged to place bike racks at stores and office buildings. Many of the regulations pertaining to bike stands on public property must be updated and streamlined if businesses in the community are to place bike racks for their employees. These racks should be made from heavy-gauge metal and placed in well-lighted public places. If not so built, the bike rack becomes a centralized rip-off depot for bike thieves.

Your bike plan for your area may be any one of the above ideas or may be a combination of all of them. It is important to get as much feedback as possible from other cyclists in your area. To do this, you might want to bring the cyclists together for a bike-in, bike rally, or even a bike convention. Putting one of these things together does not happen overnight. The following discussion should give you some idea of what's involved when you plan a bike-in or rally.

A bike-in should be planned as well in advance as possible.

The route should be gone over in detail. The police should be notified of the ride, the park authorities contacted, and provisions made for first aid. Refreshments should be available at the end of the ride and bike marshals might be used to check for stragglers or accidents. You might also have a "sag wagon" follow the group. This station wagon or truck can pick up stragglers, bikes and all, and get them to the end of the ride.

Then there's publicity. This is a whole trip in itself and should be done by someone with some experience with the media. First you should try to get publicity before the event. Appear on a TV talk show or some community show, or try to interest someone on these shows. Have posters and leaflets made and distribute them to the bike shops and playgrounds, and on major bike routes. Send a press release to all the major newspapers for insertion in any community calendars they print. Make sure you send the release to the small neighborhood papers that are published once a month or biweekly. Send public service spot announcements about the event to radio stations about two weeks in advance. You might get a public service ad on TV but this usually takes a considerable amount of time and money. Follow up the release with a phone call just before the event to see if the media got your release. Make sure to send a release to the city wire services and the national media. It can't hurt. All this should get at least some press. If you don't make page one, don't be upset – it all depends on what else happened that day. Your bike-in could always be killed by some flash from the White House. You never can tell.

Before you've managed to gather these people together, you should have a firm idea of what they are to do. Should you present an elaborate program with dignitaries or a rock band and exhibit booths? Should there be any program at all? People don't have to "do" anything. You should, however, circulate some sort of literature about the organization that put the bike-in together. You should also circulate a petition about some aspect of bicycling. This provides you with names and addresses of interested cyclists to start a mailing list and provides the officials that you present the petition to with concrete proof that people are concerned about cycling in your area. And then, when you have nothing to do, order it not to rain.

Next, you might conduct a bike census and find out where the cyclists are in your area, where they go, and what they do with their bikes once they get there. This information will be valuable in formulating your bike routes and finding out where bike racks are needed.

Take a close look at your city's bike regulations. It is important that they contain the following provisions:

Equal Rights. All persons have equal rights whether driving cars or riding bikes. Cyclists should be governed by the same laws as motorists and have the same responsibilities. Too often I've seen cyclists riding the street the wrong way, cutting in and out of traffic, and endangering themselves and those around them. These people make life more difficult for all of us.

Car Harassment. Drivers often harass cyclists by cutting the rider off, blasting their horns, throwing objects, and stopping quickly. These dangerous acts should be considered reckless driving and should be dealt with accordingly. Cyclists should be able to report license numbers of offenders to the police and expect appropriate action. (You might also be able to get the name and address of the driver from the motor vehicle bureau and deal directly with him.)

Stolen Bicycles. A list of stolen bicycles that have been reported to the police should be made available to the public. The community itself will then be able to take action against bike thieves. This vigilante-type action might also serve to deter bike thieves. In many cities recovered, but unclaimed, bikes are put up for auction by the police department. In a move to get bikes back to the people, Washington, D.C., has started a program of giving away the bikes to organizations that distribute them to people who need bikes but don't have money to pay for them.

Street Grates. Slotted grates should be installed crossways to the flow of traffic to prevent the bicycle wheel from dropping into a slot and throwing the rider over the handlebars. A number of fatalities have been recorded because of this problem. If the highway department is informed of this hazard and nothing is done, they stand liable for injuries; so it is important that they be informed.

Car Doors. The sudden opening of a car door on the street side is the nightmare of every commuting cyclist. To open a car door on the street side of a busy city street should be a traffic offense.

Right-hand Turns by Cars. Cars turning are required by law to signal before doing so. This regulation should be strictly enforced. The bicyclist on the right side of the street is at the mercy of any car making a sudden right-hand turn.

These are some of the more important regulations that are needed. There might be individual problems in your area that could require special attention. Look around and see what's going on.

Political Action in the Cities

Many cities throughout the country have come forward with various proposals aimed at promoting cycling as transportation. Concerned with the increasing air pollution and congestion, city officials have begun to realize that the car might not be an answer to their transportation problems.

The city of Davis, California, has long been a shining example of what can be done on the municipal level to encourage bicycling. In a city of twenty-four thousand people some eighteen thousand bicycles have been registered. In the early 1960s it became evident that some way was needed to separate the car and the bicycle. A citizen group was formed that circulated a petition calling on the city council to establish a system of bicycle paths along major city streets. Bike paths became a central issue in the city election in 1966 and the bike candidates won. A bike path network was developed soon thereafter. It was decided to create bike lanes on the outside of any street over fifty feet wide. Present plans call for some twelve miles of bike paths by 1974.

These bike paths in Davis have produced a number of tangible benefits for the town. It was found that even in the summer months when Davis's student population was small some 40 percent of all traffic was bicycles. During rush hours, 90 percent of all bicycle riders were adults. This extensive use of bicycles has meant that there are no parking meters in the town and that rush-hour traffic is tolerable. Because parking is not a problem for cyclists, business in the city has improved and both the city and the university have had to pave less land for parking lots.

In spite of the hills, San Francisco cyclists have developed a system of bike routes and bike paths that can really serve the city cyclist. The San Francisco Bicycle Coalition, composed of various bicycle and ecology groups, was formed to promote the bicycle for everyday transportation. It has proposed that a lane on Market Street, which is being reconstructed and beautified, be reserved for cyclists. It alerts its members to key political issues in cycling and stresses participation.

Similarly, other cities such as Boston, Chicago, Washington, D.C., Omaha, Lincoln (Nebraska), Syracuse (New York), Milwaukee, and Miami have all instituted some sort of in-city bike routes. These activities vary from posting signs and calling streets bikeways to restricting some lanes on selected streets to bikes-only lanes.

Action on the State Level

Numerous bills have been introduced in various state legislatures concerning bicycling. In Oregon, House Bill 1700, introduced by Don Stathos, was approved in May, 1971, and provides for at least 1 percent of the state highway money to be used for construction and maintenance of bike and footpaths.

At this writing in California, SB 108, introduced by Representative Mills, was passed and lies unsigned on Governor Ronald Reagan's desk. It would provide $720,000 annually to aid state agencies in funding bike and horse paths. The money would come from the state's share of the gas tax that will be collected starting July 1, 1972. This money could provide the state portion to meet any federal matching funds that might be available. If no federal funding is available, two-thirds of the cost of a project may be allocated. This bill, in conjunction with a federal bill now pending, could provide money for bike paths in needed areas of our cities.

A number of other states including Colorado, Iowa, Massachusetts, and Ohio also have pending legislation on bicycling. These bills vary, but all of them attempt to provide needed money in order to encourage bicycling as a means of transportation.

Biking and the Federal Government

On the national level, the federal government has moved to encourage bicycling in a number of ways. Most of the action has been the result of concerned cyclists, scattered throughout the bureaucracy, who have supported cycling and have helped cyclists negotiate the red tape. Since 1971, the responsibility for bicycling has been shared by the Department of the Interior, which manages the recreational aspects, and the Department of Transportation, which manages the commuter aspects.

In the Department of Transportation, bicycling will be handled by the Office of Environmental and Urban Systems, which will look into such things as bike parking in fringe parking areas and transportation terminals, and will do research into vandal-proof bike racks. As a concerned bicyclist, Secretary Volpe has actively supported exclusive right-of-ways for cyclists on city streets and his staff has been active in trying to solve some of the problems of urban commuters. In one move to encourage cycling, the Department of Transportation has told the states that Highway Trust Fund monies can be used for bike paths *in conjunction* with federal highway projects. While it is nice to include bike paths in this highway program, it really won't help bicycling. What's needed are bike paths *around* existing freeways and highways, not alongside new highways as the program proposes.

In the Department of the Interior, the Bureau of Outdoor Recreation is helping to establish more trails for single and multiple uses. Although it is dealing with the bicycle from a recreational standpoint, many of these trails can and are being used by commuters. The National Trails Systems Act of 1968 provides for three types of trails: National Scenic Trails, which are established only by Congress; Recreation Trails, which are designated by the Secretary of Interior or Agriculture; and connecting trails, which are set up locally to link the other two systems. The twenty-nine Recreation Trails, which have been designated near urban centers, seem to have the most potential for cycling.

Through these and other government agencies, certain amounts of money are available to the states for bicycling and bicycle-related activities:

Old Railroad Right-of-Ways. The Interstate Commerce Commission has instituted railroad abandonment notification with the states. Check your state house for the name and location of the A-95 metropolitan and regional office.

Highway Trust Fund. Paths can be built with this money only along highway right-of-ways, so, if it's going through, there might as well be a bike path alongside of it.

"Legacy of Parks" Program. This is authorized by the Bureau of Outdoor Recreation and these grants provide states with funds on a fifty-fifty matching basis for acquisition, development, and planning outdoor recreational areas, including bike trails.

Urban Renewal Projects. This program can make money available for rehabilitation or redevelopment of slums and blighted areas. Bike paths can be included in this program. Administered through the Community Development section of the Department of Housing and Urban Development (HUD), bike paths can account for two-thirds to three-fourths of project costs.

Open Space Program. Another program of HUD assists states in acquiring land for permanent open space. Roadways, signs, and landscaping are included in this program, and its application to bikeways should be investigated with state and local authorities. Funds are made available on a fifty-fifty matching basis.

Many of these administrative solutions are a piecemeal approach. What is really needed is exclusive financing for bike paths around major highway interchanges and freeways, linking up with the bike lanes along major city streets. A bike path should be constructed in an area where bike lanes are in use, and if it is constructed, it should be done with the minimum harm to the environment. Be sure the path is needed; we have enough pavement land already. If federal funds are used, it might be necessary for the controlling agency to file an Environmental Impact Statement (Sec. 102 of the Environmental Policy Act) describing the effect that such a project will have on the environment.

Instead of these sometimes circuitous routes, money for bike path construction should be provided on a national level from a fund such as the Highway Trust Fund. A bill introduced by Representative Koch, of New York, in the House (H.R. 9369), the Bicycle Transportation Act of 1971 would go a long way toward creating effective bike paths where they are needed. It would provide states with funds from Federal Highway Trust Fund monies for developing bicycle path and commuter systems on a fifty-fifty matching fund basis. Funds could also be used for traffic control devices, shelters, and parking facilities. Representative Koch's bill now has forty-eight co-sponsors and has been referred to the House Public Works Committee. At this writing no hearings were scheduled. California's Senator Cranston has introduced an identical bill in the Senate (S. 2440), which now has twelve Senate co-sponsors.

With all this flurry of governmental activity, it would be expected that bicycle manufacturers and traditional biking organizations would come together to exert pressure on the legislators on strong bike legislation, but this has not been the case. The traditional biking organizations, basically recreational in nature, have not really provided the leadership needed to bring cyclists together to put pressure on the powers that be. Many of their members load their cars down with bikes and roar off to the country away from the smog and congestion for a weekend of idyllic cycling. While nothing is wrong with getting away from it all on a bike, it is unfortunate that more people have not been more forceful in dealing with the problems of the city cyclist.

The bicycle industry has only relatively recently been active politically. The Bicycle Institute of America (BIA), a group of American bicycle manufacturers, has acted as spokesman for the industry. In the past it has certainly done a wonderful job acting as a resource for the biking community, supplying bike literature on many bike-related subjects, lending films, pictures, displays, and so forth. Yet in most of its literature it still seems to regard the bicycle as a toy to be used by kids — which it was for many years. But times have changed, and so have the bikes and the people who ride them. The import market is rising and many of the buyers are now adults. With this rise in the adult market, there has been a corresponding rise in the number of concerned cyclists who demand their right to use the bike as an everyday means of transportation without endangering limb or lung.

The industry has been slow to pick up on what is happening for two reasons. First of all it, like everyone else, was completely unprepared for the bike boom that now has succeeded in putting upward of eighty million Americans on two wheels. It was all it could do to make bicycles, much less keep up with the changing market patterns. Also, the industry was reluctant to directly confront some of the basic assumptions that America has developed about transportation since World War II. The bike movement already has begun to directly challenge cars for room on the streets, and from all political and social indications, the pressure for room on the road for bikers will continue to mount.

Whatever its reasons, there are now indications that BIA and its manufacturing members have begun to get more active and realize the role that the bicycle can play in transportation. With its financial and technical resources, the industry can be of tremendous help to citizen cycling groups throughout the country.

Yet even the strongest industry lobbying effort might not achieve what the commuting cyclist needs. In this country of special interests, it would be foolhardy to depend on industry to keep the wheel rolling. Recognizing a void on the national cycling scene, a number of groups have organized to focus on various aspects of bicycling.

Members of Concerned Bike Riders for the Environment, a group based in Los Angeles, are what the name implies — and more. They are a nonprofit, volunteer group working to educate the public and to implement measures that would end pollution, curb misuse and destruction of the earth's resources, and limit deterioration of the natural environment. They en-

courage bicycling by pushing for bike paths and lanes on all
major thoroughfares, bike racks at prime locations, and storage sections on public transports. They are active politically,
lobbying with county and city councils, state legislatures, and
Congress for environmentally oriented legislation.

Send $3 to become a member. Write to:

Nancy Pearlman
Concerned Bike Riders for the Environment
P.O. Box 24388
Los Angeles, California 90024
(213) 473-3211

Friends for Bikecology is another recently organized
national group concerned with bicycling and ecology. A nonprofit, volunteer group, its members think that physical and
psychological separation of the car and the bicycle is essential
to promote bicycling in meaningful ways. After organizing
National Bikecology Day rides in fifty cities throughout the
country, the organization has built its membership to over
one thousand people in less than a year. Friends for Bikecology
seeks to make a political issue out of bikeways on local, state,
and national levels. It was the first organization to deal with
the lack of bikeways on a national scale. It plans to lobby for
the use of Highway Trust Fund and gas tax revenues in building bikeways. Student membership is $3 and family member-
ship is $5. Write to:

Ken Klosbun
Friends for Bikecology
1035 East De La Guerra
Santa Barbara, California 93103
(805) 966-5698

And then there is San Luis Obispo, California, a quiet mid-
state university town, which is distinguished by not having
had a single student demonstration during the sixties (an
omission due to lethargy rather than conservatism). Late last
year, San Luis's City Council decided that bikes parked on
sidewalks were something of a nuisance, and passed a directive
to the police department to start handing out tickets.

Over the objections of cyclists pleading dangers to their
machines from automobiles and thieves, and the local Kiwanis

Club, which offered to set up one bike rack per downtown city block, the council maintained that bike riders must "obey the same laws as other vehicle riders," including parking in the street. There being none so blind as those who will not see, the council had no inkling of what was coming.

The following Thursday evening—the only evening San Luis stores are open until 9:00 P.M.—the cyclists made their move. Cruising the main business area and watching for automobiles leaving open meter spaces, the riders proceeded to tie up four hundred parking spots. The police remained true to their orders, refusing to allow motorists to remove the cycles, and in a short while, shopping was dramatically curtailed.

By December sixteenth bicycle racks were installed in the downtown area, and the city officials were busy charting bicycle paths for the militant pedalers.

Dealing with Bureaucrats

Whatever the politician legislates or the citizens' group proposes, most of the real action is usually left up to a bureaucrat of one kind or another. There are good bureaucrats and bad bureaucrats, but either way, if they don't understand what you are trying to do, they can stop the whole show as effectively as if it had never happened.

There are a number of ways to deal with this problem. The first step is to know your local bureaucrats and what they do or are supposed to do. As I have outlined earlier, you must get all the information you can about them and their jobs. By the time you have filled in most of the blanks on your Handy Bureaucrat Directory, you should have a good idea of what goes on.

Try to get as specific as possible when you deal with a bureaucrat. Don't telephone a traffic engineer and demand that bike lanes be put down every road. He will feel threatened and will have no choice but to react defensively. Instead, the first time you call him, briefly outline your proposal including how much it will cost and the benefits to be realized. The second time you call him, mention your proposal to him again, telling him why it is needed, why it will work, and most important, how much it will cost. The third time you call him, you should mention the other people who support the proposal, the media you've contacted, and the probable consequences that a wrong decision might have. Then leave the poor man alone; additional hassling can only make him resist your ideas.

When and if a decision is made, it will probably not be everything you wanted. Congratulate the man and/organization publicly for the good parts and give him/it hell for the bad. This way you, the bureaucrat, and the general public won't get the feeling that all you ever do is complain.

Often, in spite of everything, nothing seems to move. Wait just a bit longer to see if any glimmerings of action occur. If you have exhausted all bureaucratic and political possibilities, try to focus the public's attention on the problem with a number of direct actions. These actions should be thought out and well publicized when possible. Keep in mind that the government must move in moments of crisis. That the government caused the crisis or that its solution may cause another crisis doesn't really matter. The point is that the government must act in some way even if it is only of marginal value. Because there are no prepared answers in times of crisis, bureaucrats become confused and unsure of how to act. Creation of a crisis then may serve to trigger a response from a previously unresponsive bureaucracy. The following scenarios might be useful as general guidelines to focus attention on the problems of the city cyclist.

1. Ten cyclists decide to ride home on a two-lane, rush-hour road. The cyclists are forced to ride closer to the center of the lane because of potholes, glass, or general debris on the right-hand shoulder. Cars are unable or unwilling to pass and back up causing traffic jam. Drivers complain to city officials.

2. A cyclist in bumper-to-bumper traffic experiences car harassment. The cyclist catches up to motorist, takes a garden hose, and whaps the back fender of the car, scaring hell out of the driver but causing no damage to the car. Driver complains to officials.

3. This scenario is similar to the above one except that the specific car is an habitual harasser. The next day ten cyclists appear and harass the car. Driver complains to city officials.

Survival on a Bike in the City

Let us not pretend for a minute that cycling in the city is easy. It's not. It is a daily battle between you, the cars, and the air pollution. Cycling in traffic requires certain tactics to dramatically increase your survival time on the streets.

1. Keep your ears open. It's your ears that save your ass every time. You hear the cars in back of you, hear the click of the latch of the car door in front of you, hear the noises of your bike beginning to fall apart.

2. Keep looking around. You can see much farther ahead than most drivers so take advantage of that fact and take evasive actions early. Keep scanning the driver's seat of parked cars for door-opening idiots. Watch for fools who decide to take quick right turns through your front wheel.

3. Be visible. Wear one of those reflective vests. At night have a good light such as a strap-on leg lamp that has a white light in front and a red one in back. Strap it to your leg, so it moves up and down. Drivers won't dare run over you, for they won't know what has one red light and hops up and down.

4. Cuss a lot. A set of screamed cuss words seems to make people pause a little before they commit a lethal act. It is just this pause of one to two seconds that you need to get out of a difficult situation, so use this borrowed time wisely. Try to be creative in your cussing—the same old shit's not going to stop anybody. Remember, if prostitution is the oldest profession, then swearing is the oldest art.

5. Carry a copy of the bike regulations. Most people, including policemen, do not know the law. Be sure you stay in the right as much as possible—it helps if you go to court.

6. Pick your enemies wisely. I try to be selective about who I harass, leaning most heavily on rich people with big cars who have just tried to kill me. Stay away from the six-foot truck drivers, unless of course you are a six-foot-six football player who can handle it.

Keep in mind the critical point. Remember that when you are on your bike in the city you become not only a cyclist but a *transportation alternative.* Car drivers think that the streets are completely for cars and you must reeducate them to accept other sorts of vehicles on the roads that we all own. The best time for this education is during the morning and afternoon rush hours. You should pick a route and stick with it for a couple of weeks. Try to ride about the same time every day. This means that the chances of passing the same people every day are fairly high. You are providing them with an example that it is possible to escape from the Detroit madness. If you do it right, you might even become a tradition. You should take the time whenever you can to correct the faults of your pupils in cars. People must get in the habit of looking for bikes when they cross intersections, pull out of parking spaces, and open doors. Often these people have almost killed you without meaning to and are most apologetic when confronted with what they ve done. The best education for motorists is cyclists, out on the street, dealing with cars on their own territory and showing others that it can be done.

Changing attitudes is not an instant thing. You're dealing with some basic assumptions about transportation in America. The car has become as basic a part of America as rush hour and apple pie and people won't dispense with it easily. But the air-destroying, land-grabbing internal combustion engine cannot be allowed to run loose much longer. Alternatives in transportation are desperately needed if the world as we know it is to continue to survive. The bicycle can provide that alternative.

8 *Racing and Touring*

Round and round and round they go. Except when they're not involved in a track race, in which case they go in a variety of directions, though never in more than one direction at once, barring unforeseen circumstances such as accidents. It's exciting!

We can look for lots more of them going round and round right in the U.S.A. Within the next decade, expect to see bicycle racing become almost as popular here as it is in Europe. Americans have always loved daredevils, and champion cyclists are definitely in a class with Evel Knievel. Though it will probably never capture the secret heart of our nation like roller derby has, there is surely an available nook or cranny that bicycle racing might occupy.

Touring, on the other hand, is not quite so competitive and lots more fun for the average cyclist. So don't watch for it on your television set. Unless Omnibus *makes a comeback.*

Whizzing around at thirty miles an hour, six inches from another cyclist, the world rushes by at an incredible pace, yet with a grace, smoothness, and silence that cannot be duplicated on any other machine. Cycle racing requires a curious combination of brains, brawn, and masochism. Each racer must judge the skill of the other racers, the conditions, and the course and then plan when to make his move.

Cycle racing is just beginning to come into its own as an acknowledged sport in the United States. Europe, of course, has enjoyed cycle racing for a number of years. During the Tour de France, everyone pauses to catch news of the riders as they strain against the mountains, the wind, and the clock. The winners are national heroes and have their fortunes made.

Here, in the States, more and more college campuses are sponsoring cycling teams. Bike shops in all parts of the country also encourage races and meets. The First Tour of California, created by Velo Sport Cycle Shop in Berkeley, was a tremendous success. More than one hundred riders cycled some 686 miles over a ten-day period. Many of the people who saw this race were seeing a bicycle road race for the first time, an experience both pleasant and perplexing for the uninitiated.

Cycle racing is usually divided into road racing and track racing. Though each type of racing requires a different technique and a different machine, constant factors are speed, strength, and stamina.

Road racing is what the name implies and more. The road cyclist encounters many kinds of road surface and terrain. Weather conditions also affect his performance. Thus, a road bike must be carefully selected to fit any possible situation. Because of varying road conditions, a good road frame is of the utmost importance. It must be flexible, yet strong enough to hold up under stress. The frame angles should be set at about seventy-three degrees, so that the bike can absorb some of the vibration from the road. Vibration can really wear a rider down over a long distance, so it is essential that it be minimized whenever possible. The road bike should have a fairly long wheelbase and the wheels should be spoked to give resilience, not rigidity. Gears tend to be at fairly close range with gear levers mounted on the ends of the handlebars.

In road racing, the leader is usually at a severe disadvantage. He acts as a windbreak for other riders, allowing them to slipstream along with little exertion. After a while, the rested riders assume the lead while the former leaders take their places in comparative comfort near the back of the path. In this way, a group of ten riders avoids fatigue and keeps a long race going.

However, a rider can't win in the middle of the pack, nor can he maintain a lead position throughout the race. That's what makes for a bike race, to paraphrase some ancient savant. Great cyclists are those men able to analyze the myriad elements operating in any given race, and then devise a strategy that will net them a victory. They move from pack to pack or jump off to start a new pack or fall back to rest, always searching for their opening. On rare occasions, a rider may try to hold the lead for an entire race, but only if he is in peak condition.

Since riders tend to cycle in packs, a race is often decided by a "hell-for-leather" sprint at the end. It's sobering to think of cycling for a hundred miles and then sprinting for the finish, but this is generally the case. Somehow, somewhere the riders must come up with one last dollop of energy to push them past the finish line. Races are often won by a matter of inches — and can be lost in a matter of seconds. It's a long, hard road to race.

Track racing is a completely different affair. Cyclists speed around and around a banked wooden or concrete track. The track bike is built very light and sturdy with just the bare essentials. It usually has a very short wheelbase, and a solid frame with the frame angles being much larger than those of the road machine. The track bike has none of the flexibility of the road bike, nor does it have any brakes. It is built with a "fixed" wheel instead of the freewheel of the road bike, which means that coasting is impossible. This is a direct drive system like a tricycle's; the pedals move the wheel and the wheel moves the pedals. Riders stop by rubbing the front wheel with their gloved hand while trying to slow the pedals down, a precarious undertaking that delights racing enthusiasts.

There are various sorts of track and touring races. Each requires different skills and tactics.

Pursuit. In this race, the riders start at opposite sides of the track and try to catch one another. Since riders are evenly matched according to their speeds, most pursuit races never result in a capture. Best time wins.

Point Race. In either track or road races, points can be awarded to the winners of various laps. The champion obviously is the one with the highest number of points at the end of a race.

Miss and Out. A track race in which all riders start together. At the conclusion of every lap the last one or two riders must withdraw until only two contestants remain. They then sprint for the finish on the last lap.

Handicap. In either road or track races, weaker riders can be given a time or distance handicap over the stronger riders.

Time Trail. Either a track or road race against the clock.

Match Race. A track race in which riders sprint for the finish. Usually less than one thousand meters.

Training techniques for these different races vary widely

among racers. Generally, though, it is important to get as smooth a power stroke as possible. This method utilizes both body and machine strength.

The best single source of information about cycle racing in the states is the Amateur Bicycle League of America. You can contact it at:

Amateur Bicycle League of America
President, Ernest Seubert
137 Brunswick Road
Cedar Grove, New Jersey 07009

Good luck.

"Where did you go for your vacation?" asked the tall man waiting for an elevator in the Smithsonian Institution.

"Cayman Islands," replied the second.

"Where on earth are the Cayman Islands?"

"I've no idea," said the second. "We flew."

Free of the forced, hectic, pressurized competition of racing and everyday life, cycle touring is a leisurely method of relaxing the brain and stimulating the spirit. It makes the cyclist unique because he does something few people can do today; he moves at an enjoyable and natural pace, and he sensually experiences the beauty of life. How unfortunate travel is for the average American; in our hasty push for something we call progress, we reduce the complexity of our environment to the size of a car window, or we lift ourselves so far above it, its most majestic snow-capped peak appears no larger than a pubescent pimple.

And with the rapidity of our travel, we transform our environment's elegance into that of a still-life landscape painting: something to admire only at a distance, in a particular location, on certain days. We isolate ourselves from the healthy rigors of actual physical travel over long distances. Who gets sweat in their eyes and calluses on their hands from driving a car? Have you ever tried to outrace a storm on a bicycle? Do

you know how good water tastes after you've cycled the Bonne-
ville Salt Flats? And when did you last enjoy, as you traveled,
the woody smell of pine tar resin on a crisp, mountain morning,
the rhythmic sound of a woodpecker hunting for its breakfast,
and the frantic feathered vision of a wild turkey exploding
from the underbrush? These are the simple pleasures of cycle
touring.

There are two camps of cycle tourists: individuals who just
like to tour, and on long trips carry little equipment, eat in
restaurants, and sleep in motels, or have friends follow them in
a trailer filled with the necessary gear; and people who like to
rough it, haul their "homes" on their cycles, cook their own
meals, and bed down where they can. In both instances, certain
cycling ground plans exist.

The most important ground plan is the bicycle. Any type of
cycle can be ridden long distances—some stalwart fellows have
even crossed the United States on balloon-tired tanks—but
generally, the ground rule on cycles is: the better the cycle and
the more gears available to the cyclist, the easier and more enjoyable the cycling will be. Consequently, the touring cycle
should weigh no more than twenty-seven pounds, and should
have dropped handlebars, a broken-in saddle, and a wide gearing range. An ideal range for carrying weight and climbing
mountains, for example, is a rear cluster of 14, 16, 19, 24, and
28 teeth with two chainwheels of 38 and 52 teeth.

The touring cycle's tires open the wounds of argument over
the advantages and disadvantages of clincher and sew-up
tires. As described earlier, most cyclists prefer sew-ups and
light rims because of their resiliency, weight, and pedalability.
When hauling a load long distances, however, the stronger
clincher is more dependable and more available; it can be purchased in any cycle shop. The general rule for tire-type selection is: if you aren't ready to hassle with the peculiarities of
sew-ups, ride on clinchers with their steel rims. If you intend to
cycle over rough dirt or gravel roads, you must use clinchers.
If you do plan to employ sew-ups for touring, the tires should be
heavier-weight models, between twelve and fifteen ounces, and
when crossing bumpy spots on a loaded cycle fitted with sew-

ups, you should "stand" in the pedals and shift body weight to the handlebars, distributing weight equally over the wheels to lessen the possibility of tire and rim damage. Good touring sew-ups are made by Clement: the cotton Elvezia and Gran Sport, and the silk Campionato Del Mondo.

Certain accessories facilitate long-distance cycling and are important to have. Toe clips are essential, particularly when climbing steep roads on a weighted cycle. Carrying at least one water bottle (two is a better idea) is necessary. When cycling in the rain, remaining dry is difficult. Personal ingenuity is the best aid in solving this problem when it occurs, but some guidelines are: (1) equip the cycle with plastic snap-on fenders to eliminate wheel spray and wear a specially designed cycling poncho or cape, both available in quality cycle shops; (2) ride in a water-repellent parka and nylon rain chaps, both found in backpacking or mountaineering stores; (3) ride in your clothes and tolerate the wetness; (4) wear a pair of shorts or a bathing suit and groove on the hydrologic cycle; or (5) don't ride when it rains.

No chapter on touring would be complete without some comment about where and when to tour. Our directive suggestion is simple: ride wherever you personally find the beauty and serenity of nature, and whenever you feel like riding.

Because the conventional cycle tourist sleeps and eats in established places, he has little need for the more elaborate, extensive gear carried by the cycle camper. At most, the cycle tourist should carry a handlebar "day" bag — several models of which are available from the American Youth Hostels, Brooks of England, and Bellwether of San Francisco and cost between $12 and $15 — in which he can stuff a sweater, maps, bagged lunch, first-aid kit, and other odds and ends (see figures 42 and 43), and a larger rear bag for carrying the few personal possessions he will have (see figure 44). Good rear bags are made by H. W. Carradice of England, Bellwether, and models available from the Youth Hostels; their cost is from $15 to $20. For hauling the bags, the cycle should be fitted with a front T.A. bracket, found in most cycle shops (costs about $5), that protects the center-pull brakes, or if the cycle's head-tube is too long, with a Schwinn-made alloy front bag carrier. On the rear should be the dependable Pletscher rack found in cycle shops everywhere.

Panniers are the larger equipment-carrying bags used by the camping cyclist. Several front and rear models are made, the best by Carradice, Bellwether, and Bergen of Norway, which are carried by the Youth Hostels. These bags are usually of canvas, though Bellwether is of lightweight, water-repellent nylon, are sectioned for efficient weight distribution, and are shaped to hang from steel-rod racks over the front and rear wheels. (See figure 45.) These bags cost from $20 and $30 and can hold a lot of equipment.

Unlike the cycle tourist who carries little "survival" equipment, the cyclist camper, to comfort himself against nature's elements, needs to transport gear that is of the highest utility value, yet is lightweight and easily storable.

The first piece of equipment on his list should be a good sleeping bag. The type to get is mummy-shaped, weighs about three pounds, is completely down-filled, baffled, and employs a differential cut (meaning the inside nylon shell is smaller than the outside for efficient heat retention). This bag will keep the camper comfortable in temperatures down to fifteen degrees. It costs about $90 and can be stuffed down to eighteen inches by seven inches. Excellent examples of this bag are the Sierra Design Model 100, and the North Face Superlight.

A sleeping bag must be kept from the cold and damp of the ground, so an insulator is necessary. Lightweight air-mattresses are excellent for this and are comfortable to boot. Stebco makes a reliable mattress that weighs 1 pound, 12 ounces, is forty-nine inches long, and costs $10. Superlightweight Ensolite pads three-quarters of an inch thick are also good insulators, but they are bulkier and harder to pack than air mattresses.

As one worldly wanderer said, "The best roof for your bedroom is the sky." Consequently, a tent shouldn't be toted. Not only do tents separate you from nature but also their bulkiness and weight make them difficult to transport. Of course, there are times when some kind of shelter is necessary, and in these instances the best article to have is a tube tent — nothing more than an easily folded, large, single-piece polyethylene (or

Figs. 42 and 43: Because he carries little equipment, the conventional cycle tourist doesn't need large bags. Bellwether Sporting Goods of San Francisco makes excellent tourist "day" bags that fit on the handlebars or behind the saddle. The handlebar bag is particularly practical because when removed it serves as a shoulder pack.

Fig. 44. An ideal tourist rear bag is the Bellwether model #1202. In it the tourist rider can stuff the few clothing articles and odds and ends he carries.

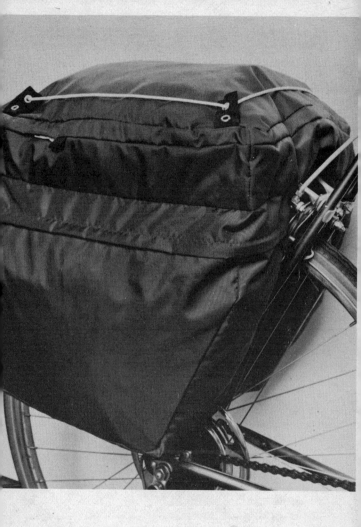

Fig. 45. The "Grand Touring Pack" by Bellwether is an excellent example of the pannier bags carried by the cycle camper. Made of lightweight, durable, waterproof nylon, the bags are designed for maximum storage capacity and fit any rear carrying rack. They cost $30.

nylon) sheet, open at both ends. These tube tents are handy to have in rainstorms, they're easy to put up (they hang from a nylon cord stretched between two trees), and they keep you less wet than being in the rain; but they do have problems. Sleeping in one is like sleeping in a plastic bag (you feel like some Bird's-Eye vegetable ready for the pot), and they can't stand heavy abuse. They weigh about one and one-half pounds and cost about $2. For those individuals who prefer to take a tent there are models available from sporting goods stores and backpacking outfitters that will serve your purpose.

Easily portable stoves are more reliable, more efficient, and more controllable than campfires for cooking. Svea, Primus, Bluet, all make superb lightweight stoves. The Svea 123 and Primus 711 burn white gas, and the Bluet 200 uses a disposable butane cartridge. All weigh less than two pounds and cost less than $10. White gas, which is easily found in rural areas, can be carried in special lightweight aluminum or plastic containers. Since the wise cycle camper selects a bedroom near stores and markets, the only food carried long distances should be staples (salt, pepper, fruit, and the like) or easily packed energy snacks. Mess kits and cooking gear should be of polished aluminum.

Like everything else, clothing carried should be light but efficient. Here is a list that may help you in deciding what to take:

2 pairs shorts
1 pair long pants
2 cycling jerseys (or light knit shirts)
sweat pants
sweater (or sweat shirt)
down jacket
nylon rain parka or poncho (parka doubles as windbreaker)
2 pairs socks
sunglasses
cycling hat
gloves (optional)
bandanna
tennis shoes
cycling shoes (optional)

Miscellaneous cycle camping gear includes:

> small Mallory flashlight with alkaline batteries
> leg lamp with alkaline batteries
> nylon cord
> soap
> spoon
> knife
> sunburn lotion
> waterproof match carrier
> bike tent — protecting plastic sheet available from cycle shops
> elastic shock cords

Tools that should be carried depend in part on how long and how far the cyclist intends to ride. For trips lasting more than a month, the following tools and spare parts will be needed for complete bicycle overhauls; for trips less than a month, of course, many of these items can be eliminated:

> chain rivet remover and spare chain links
> cone wrenches
> crescent wrench
> pliers
> 6″ screwdriver
> metric hex key (5 mm)
> Mafac tool kit
> spare derailleur cable
> spare brake cable
> 6 spare spokes
> spoke wrench
> 4 spare brake pads
> 2 spare brake shoes
> freewheel remover
> crank extractor (for cotterless cranks)
> bicycle grease
> small can of light oil
> tire patch kit
> 2 spare sew-ups
> 1 spare inner tube (for clincher)
> 2 tire irons (clincher tires)

The amount of weight to be carried is entirely up to the individual cyclist, but it's best to travel as light as possible, carrying only those items that are basic to survival. The American Youth Hostels advise that the limit of weight carried over the rear wheel should be twenty pounds; this is because rear tires and rims are susceptible to damage from weight when bounced over bumpy roads.

At first, riding a loaded cycle is tricky business. For safer and easier cycling, practice riding your loaded cycle before actually starting on your trip. The best method is to ride daily for a month prior to leaving and, each day, increase the distance you pedal. As you'll discover, sharp turns call for slower speeds, climbing big hills necessitates down-shifting sooner, and going down steep hills requires early braking to avoid speed build-up and possible wipe-outs.

One final word of advice: if you're planning any kind of extended cycle tour, you should do just that: *plan.* Gather as much information and think of as many ideas as you possibly can concerning your trip. Aids for planning can be found in the following:

For campground locations and information, Rand, McNally puts out a *Guide to Campgrounds* that costs about $2 and contains in-depth descriptions of campsites.

For maps and possible routes contact the AAA; it has piles of material, and if you're a member, AAA will be more than willing to help you chart your route (it once helped a guy who was going to ride a Pogo stick from Washington, D.C., to Chicago). Additional maps can be secured from the Department of Interior or a state highway department. Having county maps that show little-used, paved, alternate roads is important to the cyclist.

Writing to the American Youth Hostels and the League of American Wheelmen is helpful. The AYH publishes a *North American Bicycle Atlas,* which describes and locates bicycle routes, tours, and paths in North America.

Visiting your local cycle club and, especially, your local bicycle shop, is wise. The people who run and staff these organizations are avid cyclists and will know of places to go and things to expect on cycle tours. Reading Colin Fletcher's *The Complete Walker* is good for information concerning lightweight, efficient camping equipment.

Remember: the key to survival on a bicycle is being ready for anything that may occur. This does not mean you must be paranoid, just, as the old Scout slogan says, "Be prepared."

May the wind always be at your back . . . ride on!

9 *British Cycling*

PETER LAWLOR

*This chapter is about the bicycling experience in Great Britain.
I can say no more.*

I arrived in England, leaving my past bike behind in California. One can leave a bike, for though it is faithful, it does not whimper.

I could have taken it, as did my young friend, Robin Collier, who rode right across the U.S., unflipped his quick-release hubs at New York airport, parceled it all into a nylon bag, paid no extra freight to Europe, and then, on he went.

What's the point, though? It's only taking coals to Newcastle. Of course, Robin loved his bike because he had all his idiosyncrasies built in. But there's a world of bikes here, and reasonable too.

Buying a bike "right off the peg," as they call it, is a simple matter. The tourist flying to London on a month charter has no problem. The yellow pages in the telephone directory yield a multitude of shops. Look under "Cycle," not "Bicycle," just the same way as you will look under "Car," not "Automobile." The English are to the point in terminologies.

As it takes some kind of a genius to handle the phones, don't call up, just go there. Even simpler yet, go to Lillywhites in Piccadilly, right in the heart of London. There, elegant, elderly gentlemen who look as though they have never ventured far from a croquet field will serve you and discuss in a soothing knowledgeable manner the exact sort of machine you require. Do not be disturbed by the life-sized photo of Eddy Merck, hot from the Tour de France, or the glare on the hippopotamus head over the gun department: you are here to be helped.

In quiet tones, the points will be gone over. The gear ratio will be worked on in a notebook discreetly drawn from behind the breast-pocket kerchief. Even the tension of the leather in the saddle will not escape notice, for where a gentleman sits is important. Though price is seldom mentioned, you will be paying no more than anywhere else in London.

Buying the practical sportsman's machine, a lightweight with mostly English parts, will cost no more than $75 U.S. equivalent. It will have a Simplex or Huret derailleur—five speeds. The rear sprocket cluster will not be the enormous kind you climb the side of a wall with; the English cyclist is Spartan and maintains there are not that sort of hills in England.

By all means go American and ask for a front derailleur for ten speeds that can be equipped with an alpine sprocket. It will cost a bit more but it will still be a bargain because the same machine will cost at least 20 percent more in the U.S.

Even ask for your special astrological color. An eyebrow is never raised in the hallowed walls of this sportsman's confessional. Remember, here is where the grouse hunter buys his shooting stick, the Ascot-goer his binoculars; this is close stuff.

English sporting goods shops are the home of personal attention. Go into the smaller cycle shops and the owner will come out and settle down for a good old talk. There is no price on words. Customers will come in and walk out unattended while he is telling you the best type of saddlebag in which to take your Thermos for an afternoon jaunt to Southend. He will tell you the route and almost take you there.

I went into one shop before I got my present bike and asked if they handled rentals. "Sorry, we don't do rentals," the owner said, "but hang on a minute, I've got a Moulton you can have for the day. Do try and get it back by the evening." It turned out it was his own bike and he used it for commuting.

Despite opportunities to shop on the Continent, I still waited to buy my bike in England because I like to talk bikes, and they will talk bikes until you are blue in the face, and you don't have to hesitate over a word. Then there are the English roads, and nothing beats them for the fun of cycling.

The bicycle boom hit England in a different way than the United States. There is no noticeable number of new cyclists on the road. There are no urgent signs for Bicycle Trail This

Way with a wiggling finger. There are no police warnings of
international bicycle rings stealing hundreds of machines.
There might be a few more businessmen cycling in London,
but not enough to raise the weathered English eyebrow. Oxford and Cambridge still remain the classic centers of gentleman cycling where the dons wheel their erratic way, gowns
dangerously flapping in the spokes. The classic ride is from one
university to the other, taking a day by all the back roads.

Look around in the shops and there are plenty of shiny, new
bicycles. There are no gaps in the display — Moultons are as
plentiful as pigeons. The fact that even the auto parts dealers
display a good rack full of roadsters, five-speeds, and ten-
speeds seems to indicate there is no shortage due to an increased demand.

But go into the firm of H. Fish and Son, for several genera-
tions purveyors to the racing cyclist who builds his own machine right from the straight tubing, charting his leg length,
weight, capabilities, and the like, and ask the firm to put you
together your own machine straight away. It is, "Sorry, sir,
but there it is. Just what there is on the floor. We can't get any
more parts. They are all going to America. If you want us to
make up a bike, it will be six months."

As they are guaranteed a certain delivery, there will be
ready-made cycles on the floor for some time but certainly not
enough to take care of a sudden, mad consumer race. Nor is it
likely that the local market will go wild. Mass hysteria is not
inherent in the British character. And they certainly regard
the American boom as hysteria. Nor is mass production the
end aim of the English cycling industry, though admittedly,
the Raleigh company, which is the biggest bicycle manufacturer in the world, has learned to get them through fast, and
produces its lower-priced models along a pretty swift belt.

No, at the heart of the island's cycling industry is quality:
the hand-built frame, the center frame and forks made only
from Reynolds 531 tubing. It is paper-thin and unmistakably
pings to the tap while others clonk. It is the strongest and the
second lightest, beaten only by French Columbus tubing.

The shortage of tubing is the main bugbear to the lightweight industry. "The manufacturers cannot meet the demand

without affecting quality," and they would never do that. Integrity does not go down the drain in this country that produced Rolls Royce.

Holdsworth, the top lightweight makers of frames, reports sudden desperate calls from American retailers. "One morning we had three phone calls before the shop opened. The first one rang wanting ten thousand bikes. The second time when the call came we asked the operator what was going on as it was still only 6:30 A.M. 'You're lucky. It's 2:00 A.M. here,' she said."

"We're beginning to educate the American market," said another maker of custom-made frames, recalling triumphantly how he talked a man from Salt Lake City into ordering ten complete bikes for one month in the following year instead of two hundred. Johnny Berry, a frame builder for fifty years, makes custom machines for championship racers and says, "At the present time I have orders for forty frame sets, six of these are for the States. I even had one American fly over especially to collect a complete machine he had ordered." And that is a good indication of the demand for craftsmanship.

With all this, somewhat of a language barrier crops up and a supplier is bothered because his gear levers are called "stick shifts" and his gears are called "cog swappers." "All they seem to want are large frames and long stems. They must be all giants over there."

And so it goes with the heart of the matter, the British frame maker, cutting, brazing, building in rigidity here and flexibility there, and all reporting increases of 70 to 90 percent in production and somehow making it without losing his touch.

I rather like Allins of Croydon, a bike shop in the old tradition, which refuses to get carried away. The shop produces only three frames a week, refusing to work in anything but 531 tubing. Allins has tried to keep his ridiculously low price of $50 for a custom road racing frame set by cutting out, as he puts it, "the fancy bits."

"You won't see any mopeds in our window," he says. "No trendy stuff here, and I don't want the headache of the export trade. I once built a tandem for a visitor, and we never heard the end of it. So many bits and pieces. And I had to please two people."

Certainly the exact opposite of mass production, Allins will build you a frame on your specifications if you'll wait up to four months, because as well as frame building, he finds he has to cope with a lot of customers, especially the type from the venerable old Cycling Touring Club (founded, 1878) who drop in and say, "Reenamel this, please, and I need a slot for my dynamo on the forks, and would you braze a bit on here first."

Well, I got my cycle in England, and all the bits were already braised on. I am particularly happy with a bit that is braised on the front fork resembling a wart. My efficient British lantern goes on that and the bulb never wavers or cuts out, and the battery lasts forever. The other brazings stop my pump from slipping off and my gears from creeping down the frame. I am particularly pleased with my luggage carrier, which doesn't slip under weight because there is a plate that stands it up from the rear brake bolt. I was brainwashed into a five-speed simply through being made to feel a bit of a softie. "Those chaps over there don't even know where their six to nine gears are. They just have to have it flashy," I was told.

Though I have become stoical about it all, and do enjoy not having to muck about with the chainwheel derailleur, which a five doesn't have, I sure could use that missing tenth gear.

But the main reason I got my bike in England is because the roads seem right for the cyclist. I find a hamlet, I find a church, I find a pub. I am never bored. The world is not being immediately spoiled before my eyes. There is the Council for the Protection of Rural England to see to that.

The motorways (freeways) are the only threat. They are not supposed to be cycled on, though you never see any prohibiting notices. The "No No" signs show up on bridleways and footpaths because it is then protecting the underdog who happens to be, in this case, the pedestrian or horse.

I hardly need the motorways because the network of roads, lanes, and byways covers every square mile of the country. It is possible to get to any point using a secondary or third-class road.

I never feel pushed off the road when I'm on a trip. Traffic moves slower and vehicles generally are smaller than in America. A mini goes by without the blast of a hundred horses from its tail pipe. A Rolls or a Bentley purrs by with the class of Cleopatra going down the Nile—and as silently. Even a semi doesn't eject me threateningly onto the shoulder with his blast of air; he moves a little quieter because he hasn't a whole continent to cross, I suppose.

There are not the bikeways that are becoming so well developed in America. The cities—apart from the one town of Stevenage, which was laid out with separate cycleways five years ago as a study, and the classic situation of Oxford and Cambridge, which have always been bicycle towns—are a hodgepodge of increasing cars and cyclists trying to hold their own. But the rural areas are perfect as they are.

Sometimes I feel like an ordinance surveyor going over the weblike maps. The turn signs leave me with a question mark for a mile or two, until the next sign, which might get me doubling back. But there is a benevolent feeling that I haven't experienced anywhere else. I think it is best summed up in a line from my handbook put out by the British Cycling Bureau, a public relations organization from the cycling industries that has been responsible for bringing cycling back: "If you see an open gate, close it."

You are in compact, tidy countryside most of the time. A farmer's field is approximately the same size anywhere; there is a hedge, there is a gate. You make sure his cattle don't get out; they can cause damage on the highway. He does not ever post his land "Keep Out." Very often there is a right of way through his land. You can use his gate, but you help him too. In return, he will not throw you out and set the dogs on you if you happen to be tired and put your sleeping bag down just inside his hedge.

I rather like these words from a handbook on right-of-ways. It makes me feel secure after being whistled, hustled, and practically shot at in some wide open fields on the other side of the Atlantic. "We hope that everyone will help to keep the paths clear. They are all public. Though the land is all owned by somebody, you have a firm—a most important—right to use the paths. Many of them are at least seven hundred years old, and men have died for this liberty. If anything blocks the path, you may remove the obstruction, or make any reasonable detour. Although you may cut barbed wire and the like, which hampers your right-of-way, we would not advise it, as straying cattle could cost a farmer dear."

So everybody helps, and if I am standing with my mouth open at a village cross road, a couple of words to anyone will bring a volume of instructions. They like doing it, and generally a bystander will join in.

It's all these things that add up to make it a no-threat world for the cyclist on the British roads.

Always I am helped too by the British Cycling Bureau. This is an organization that was founded in 1965 to keep abreast of all that is happening in the world of cycling. It is at the disposal of press and private individuals to answer questions and give advice. It has compiled over one hundred tours in England, Wales, and Scotland covering scenic spots and local history, from the undulating hills of the south to the more rugged scenery of the northern counties. It is all free. Several of the bureau's tours take the cyclist to the Continent, around The Hague, Amsterdam, Bruges, and Boulogne, and a particularly interesting one through the vineyards of the Champagne country. The latest is a grand tour of Denmark, taking in Jutland, Zealand, and Funen—three weeks in all.

I wish I had availed myself of their help when I made a trip from Amsterdam to Rotterdam, dodging around the back roads and dikes, because I was continually running into the skewered-cyclist sign forbidding pedalers on the freeways. And you don't sneak by with it there. Still, I did discover a lot of good Dutch pubs that I might have otherwise missed, and they are every bit as happy as the British ones.

If it hadn't been for the British Cycling Bureau, which was begun when the usually solid cycle industry was deep in a slump, things wouldn't have picked up for years. "First of all, we had to remove the social stigma of the bicycle," said its spokesman. "People would see a chap on a bike and jump to the conclusion that he was too poor to buy a car. So the first thing we did was to photograph Lady So and So on a bike taking flowers to the church fete, then circulate the publicity. Then it was 'Who cares what the Joneses say' after that.

"From there it was just a matter of photographing a lot of leggy birds on shiny new bikes and people started to say, That's for us. We publicized the Moultons with the new little wheels and it was the new scientific look, quick acceleration, and suspension to flatten out the bumps. Now it is all swinging back again to the lightweights and large wheels. It will probably end up where you chaps are—everybody out on the physical fitness bit—ecology, and all that."

A further boost for the industry came from the Duke of Edinburgh Award, which covers many forms of outdoor activity, especially anything of an adventurous nature. The small-wheeled bicycle captured the award with the first model in 1965 for being a new departure on the cycle horizon. The new superlightweights have been nominated for the coveted award. Awards also can be won by young cyclists in Adventure Week, which is part of the Duke's program.

This variety of organized encouragements is typical of England, where organizations thrive. "You don't have to join a club to enjoy cycling. It's an activity that calls for independence. . . . but there might be one that caters well to your particular interest," says my handbook. "There is the BCF, the ESCA, the RRA, and a welter more."

Well, you get two Englishmen playing a game of tiddledywinks and they form a club; but there is one desirable group, the Cyclists Touring Club, which is old and venerable and impinges not one iota on the cyclist's independence. You can wear plus fours and a Sherlock Holmes hat and not stir anyone. It has a large membership of twenty-two thousand, and is a little like the Triple A in that it will personally plan any route for you. There are a lot of low-priced hostels maintained by CTC, and it is affiliated with numerous farmhouses, which display the CTC sign and give a reasonable price on bed and breakfast for its members.

I would advise anyone coming over to England cycle bent not to bend his back with luggage. By all means bring a sleeping bag if you like it under the stars, and do take me literally about the farmer's field. But you are going to like the bed-and-breakfast places; they are cheap and everywhere. Sometimes you just see B and B in small letters on the side of a house. In a car you might never see it. In England, it's difficult trying to find a breakfast place by itself, though in Europe you can always find the cafés with the inevitable croissants and cheese and coffee. So it is B and B or bring a burner and pan if you're going to bag it. You just won't find a café open early out in the country.

I have always carried far too many clothes for the English climate, and on a bike I need even less. The dismal ones have told me to bundle up. My main item of use has been a brightly colored waterproof anorak. Nearly all the things I need fit into a medium-sized backpack, and I carry a hand overnight bag for respectability at immigration stops. If the sleeping bag is inevitable, I stash it away well within.

Where is the bicycle thief? Well, he hasn't found me. The stealing of bikes, like the stealing of skis, seems to belong to an affluent society. I bought a neat little lock several months ago that was guaranteed to be a case-hardened steel chain. I used it the day I bought it and haven't since. My machine sits out in its lonely glory while I go into a pub and I never worry about it.

If I saw a great multitude of bikes suddenly appearing and kids around with much more of things than they ever needed and cars perched on top of each other for want of space, I believe then I would lock my bike. It would be the point of affluence. If bikes are needed and obviously useful to the owner, then "you don't pinch a bloke's bike." I believe in some of the larger cities there is a theft problem that has arisen since bicycles have become more exotic and gone up in retail value. There you are – affluence!

Talking to some of the insurance companies, they allege to be going a bit into the red on cycle claims mainly because of their increased value and theft. The reports of thievery seemed quite bizarre compared with America. A bike is often stolen on the run, and is literally knocked from under the rider and swept away by a stronger pedaler.

One claims adjuster suspects a ring of thieves who gather the bikes up in a van to sweep them off to a waiting boat and ship them to the Middle East where cycles are in great demand. You can fit several hundred bikes on a launch just by stripping the wheels, handlebars, and pedals.

The bicycle thief is a classic figure who seems to have appeared in the course of history to supplant the horse thief. Certainly he will never be punished by death. If cycle theft comes as a result of having too much of everything, it will only be punished by boredom.

There is not yet the point of affluence to be seen here.

If all this adds up to a tight little island of protected industry, benevolent clubs, and courteous good days between cyclists, drivers, farmers, and innkeepers, it could be just that, except for the cities.

Though the countrysides don't need it, the cities will have to improve cycleways if the businessmen are bent on improving their physiques. London is a long way behind Amsterdam or Copenhagen, where the cycle commuter sits securely in the saddle and the cars respect him. It is a long way behind American cities in their closing off of parks for the sole use of bicycles.

As far as racing goes, the flair and color of European road racing is way ahead of the British. The noncycling public gets quite disturbed if a few roads are closed off for a race. The annual Milk Race, the biggest amateur road race of the year, makes it. But that is only because it is sponsored by the state Milk Board and people take it when the bureaucracy gives the word.

The one thing that bothers me is the naïveté of the motorists who believe that the new motorways being constructed will solve all their problems and create prosperity in the far corners. They should see that already in summer there's a ghastly shambles in the once lovely places served formerly by trains and winding roads. Just what does it take to show the vast hordes where it all ends up?

In this way, I think that parts of America are a long way ahead in perception. That was a long way around too—it had to be ruined first before it was turned around and improved.

Meanwhile, I'll pick Britain as the best bicycle country because, as yet, it is nonthreat. And they may even save the whole works. If the ticket man on the train allows me to nestle my bike, whole, unwrapped, and gleaming into the luggage van, and gives me a half-price ticket marked Child, I know there is still hope.

And, if I need a bespoke bike, this is where I would get it, rather than in Europe. How could I possibly explain to a gentleman in the exotic bicycle shop in, say, Milan, "I would like a bit braised on here, please"? We would all wave our arms. He would become quite hysterical.

Biographies

HAL AIGNER is primarily a film reviewer for the national magazine, *Take One,* and the Bay Area's *Night Times.* Besides a penchant for bicycling, he is a compulsive gardener with a burning ambition to grow one-hundred-pound pumpkins. This season looks very good.

LUCKY WENTWORTH was born, raised, and educated in Washington, D.C., in a no-car family. He is at present research director of the Washington Ecology Center, though he hopes to star in a soon-to-be-made feature-length film entitled *I Was a Teen-aged Bike Mechanic.*

BOB JENSEN is the chief Zen mechanic of the Zucchini Bike Shop, an organic homegrown organization whose motto is, We squash prices. He is proprietor and head craftsman of Every Sun's Mother Backyard Bed and Boomerang Factory in Berkeley, California.

CHARLIE POWERS is a bicycling cosmographer who cycled from his hometown of Bethesda, Maryland to San Francisco, where he is presently office boy for *Clear Creek* magazine. His future plans are to combine the pleasures of cycling and backpacking on a six-thousand-mile return trip this summer and to write a book about it called *Jimmy Olsen Ankles East.*

What is Clear Creek Magazine?

Thanks for asking. We are, in our humble opinion, America's liveliest environmental monthly. For example:

) *Clear Creek* broke through the previously impenetrable Lead Curtain with an article in our May, 1971 issue. We forced the government to release two suppressed reports on lead poisoning that contained frightening statistics. The city of Los Angeles formally commended us for our work. *Clear Creek* then tackled Boise-Cascade's "recreation developments" exposing their fraudulent sales-pitch and helping governments to press legal action against that behemoth. *Clear Creek* regularly publishes Nader-Raider research such as Keith Roberts' "California Water Fraud" and Cecil Fox's "Hexachlorophene, Phantom Of The Soap Opera."

) But *Clear Creek* does not confine itself solely to raking muck. We have regular featured articles covering the full spectrum of what our editor, Pennfield Jensen, calls the "Biorenaissance." Articles such as John Lewallen's "Pentagon Ecology," Michael McClure's "Wolf Net," and general features on the Asian Environment, the Russian Ecology Movement, County Government (A Manifesto for Citizen Counterevolution), Bicycling, the United Nations and Organic Merchants. We devoted our entire November issue to animal behavior, "Ethology, The Last Science." Poetry, fiction and feature writing by the best of America's environmental writers regularly grace our pages.

) Standard features calculated to lift your spirits and brighten your outlook include: Organic Gardening and Careful Cooking; Chuck Miller's incredible center-spread illustration of the "Life Form Of The Month" (Crocodiles, Nematodes, Mountain Meadows, Mollusks — all living creatures are potential material); and neat eco-alternative features like Peter Lawlor's "Birth of the Brews" (how to brew and enjoy your own stout, ale and beer).

) Reader involvement is a big part of *Clear Creek.* "What You Can Do" — it's on page one, the phone numbers, addresses, suggestions which will answer the eternal problem of what to do about environmental deterioration. Eco-Tactics is a section where our readers give their solutions to problems such as unwanted junk mail (mail back a brick with the first class postage) or how to set up a chain letter. Letters, classified and free classified ads are regular additions.

We're only one year old. If we listed everything we've done, you'd never believe us. Fortunately, *Clear Creek* will run out of material only after we have stopped pollution, raised the quality of life, and made the planet safe for man *and beast.* There's a lot of work to do and we hope that you will join the effort by reading about and supporting the men and women on the environmental firing lines around the world, the men and women you read about in *Clear Creek.*